# Hypertext
# Hands-On!

## IMPORTANT NOTES ABOUT THE SOFTWARE VERSION

Addison-Wesley can provide only limited user support for the software version of *Hypertext Hands-On!* **Instructions for using the software appear in this printed version of the work (pp. 127–130),** and you should read these instructions carefully before doing anything with your diskettes. In the event you encounter any difficulty installing or running the software, you should also refer to the appendix on user questions (pp. 130–132) or to the Read.Me file included in the software (You can use the DOS command **TYPE READ.ME** to display this file on your screen, and the command **PRINT READ.ME** to print a copy on your printer). If you are unable to find the solution to your problem in any of these places, or you have received defective diskettes, you may write or call:

Addison-Wesley Publishing Company
Customer Service
Reading, MA 01867
1-(617)-944-3700

See Addison-Wesley's warranty statement on the copyright page of this book.

**Purchasers should make backup copies of the *Hypertext Hands-On!* diskettes before doing anything else. Please note that these copies are for purchasers' own use only; it is a violation of copyright law to give or to sell copies to anyone else.**

The software version of *Hypertext Hands-On!* has been written with the *Hyperties*™ authoring system, but includes only that part of the system needed for reading. You will need the complete system in order to write your own works in hypertext format. To obtain more information about *Hyperties*, you should write or call:

Cognetics Corporation
55 Princeton-Hightstown Road
Princeton Junction, N.J. 08550
1-(609)-799-5005
1-(800)-999-1779 (orders only)

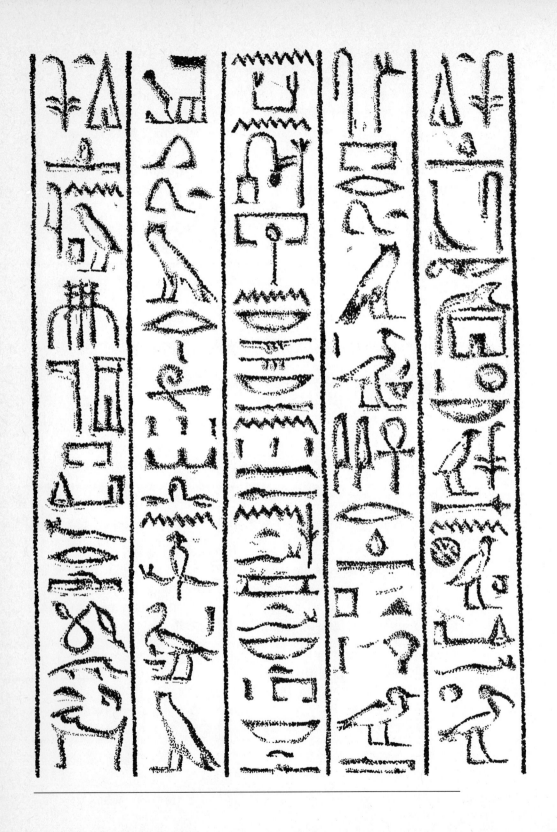

# Hypertext Hands-On!

## An Introduction to a New Way of Organizing and Accessing Information

Ben Shneiderman
and Greg Kearsley

 **Addison-Wesley Publishing Company**
Reading, Massachusetts    Menlo Park, California    New York
Don Mills, Ontario    Wokingham, England    Amsterdam
Bonn    Sydney    Singapore    Tokyo    Madrid    San Juan

| | |
|---|---|
| Sponsoring Editor | Peter Gordon |
| Production Administrator | Juliet Silveri |
| Text Design | Jean Hammond |
| Text Composition | Publication Services, Inc. |
| Cover Design | Marshall Henrichs |
| Cover Production | Jean Seal |
| Manufacturing Supervisor | Lu Anne Piskadlo |

**Library of Congress Cataloging-in-Publication Data**

Shneiderman, Ben.
 Hypertext Hands-On!: An Introduction to a New Way of Organizing and
 Accessing Information / Ben Shneiderman, Greg Kearsley.
  p.  cm.
 Bibliography: p.
 Includes index.
 ISBN 0-201-13546-9
 1. Hypertext systems.  2. IBM Personal Computer—Programming.
 I. Kearsley, Greg, 1951-  .  II. Title.
 QA76.76.H94S26    1989                                88-14662
 005.75′4—dc19                                         CIP

# The Road Not Taken

Two roads diverged in a yellow wood,
And sorry I could not travel both
And be one traveler, long I stood
And looked down one as far as I could
To where it bent in the undergrowth;

Then took the other, as just as fair,
And having perhaps the better claim,
Because it was grassy and wanted wear;
Though as for that the passing there
Had worn them really about the same,

And both that morning equally lay
In leaves no step had trodden black.
Oh, I kept the first for another day!
Yet knowing how way leads on to way,
I doubted if I should ever come back.

I shall be telling this with a sigh
Somewhere ages and ages hence:
Two roads diverged in a wood, and I—
I took the one less traveled by,
And that has made all the difference.

*Robert Frost*

# Preface

From time to time, new ideas come along that dramatically change the nature of computing. Hypertext is such an idea. It is a powerful new way of organizing and accessing information that could affect all forms of computer use.

What makes hypertext so important is that it introduces two fundamental changes in the way we store and retrieve data. The first is the capability to move rapidly from one part of a document to another by means of an associative link. The sequential pattern of reading so familiar from the print world is replaced by a truly interactive format.

The second fundamental change lies in the sharing of information across different machines and systems. Hypertext builds upon the advances made in networking to provide transparent access to data regardless of where it is located. In short, hypertext is about connectivity, within and across databases.

Ironically, hypertext is far from being a new idea. It was first proposed in 1945, predating the emergence of computers by a few years. But there are good reasons why hypertext had such a long gestation period. Hypertext demands a certain degree of computing power, storage, graphics, user interface and networking sophistication that has only recently become widely available. Hypertext is an idea that has been waiting for the technology to catch up since 1945.

This book provides an introduction to hypertext with a special twist. That special twist is a hands-on opportunity to learn about hypertext while actually using it. We have created the same information in both print and program forms so you can discover the role played by interaction in hypertext. The program is contained in two floppy disks that are affixed to the back cover of this book. An IBM PC or compatible is required to run the program. The appendix explains how to use the software.

*Hypertext Hands-On!* is intended for a wide variety of people. It should be useful to anyone involved in the computer field, whether a software engineer, system analyst, or data processing specialist. It should also be helpful to individuals involved in the fields of publishing, information science, marketing, public relations, museum, corporate training, or education who want to assess the potential impact of hypertext on their work.

*Hypertext Hands-On!* is not intended to be a course text or reference guide about hypertext, although it may be useful for these purposes in some cases. It is meant to provide a concise and practical introduction to the subject of hypertext. We therefore make no claims to completeness. Nor is the software included a complete hypertext system; it is designed to let you browse, or read through, a typical hypertext database. Readers who wish to build their own databases will need to acquire an authoring system like the ones described in this book. The authoring system that we used for the program which is included with this book is Hyperties.

A few words about the difference between the book and the software are in order. In both the printed and software forms of *Hypertext Hands-On!*, links are indicated by words or phrases in bold type. In the program, you simply select the link and you will immediately see the new information; in the book, you must turn to the indicated page number by hand. The book also features words and phrases in italics—these are glossary entries. There are many illustrations in the book that are not found on the disk because of the display limitations of the IBM PC. On the other hand, the disk contains some computer graphics and interactive examples that cannot be illustrated via print.

We would like to acknowledge the help of many people in the development of this book, including all of those involved in the Hyperties project at the University of Maryland, Charles Kreitzberg and the staff of Cognetics, Robin Halley of Park Row, and our editor at Addison-Wesley, Peter Gordon. We especially would like to acknowledge the suggestions of reviewers Christine Borgman, Richard Rubinstein, Kathleen Swigger, Trudy Bellardo, Ellen Chaffin, and Debbie Lafferty.

We hope you find *Hypertext Hands-On!* an interesting and enlightening experience.

B.S.
G.K.

# Contents

**Introduction**   xix

**1**   **Essential Concepts**   1

Overview   2
Definitions: Hypertext terminology unraveled   3
Links: The glue that holds hypertext together   3
Nodes: Units of information   5
Hierarchies: Structuring the nodes and links   6
Databases: Getting organized   7
Windows: Multiple views   9
Browsing: Exploring a hypertext system   10
Direct Manipulation: See and point interfaces   11
Indexing: Making order of the chaos   11
Searching: Finding something   12
Filters: Narrowing the search   13
Tours: Down the yellow brick path   14
Bookmarks: Electronic placemarkers   14
Path History: Keeping track and going back   15
CD-ROM: Storage for the masses   15

## 2    Applications  19

Overview    20
Dictionaries: Lexicographical links    21
Encyclopedias: Linking up knowledge    22
Medical Textbooks: Diagnostic tools    23
Product Catalogs: Let your fingers do the walking    25
Creative Writing: Interactive fiction    27
Help Systems: Context-sensitive assistance    28
Technical Documentation: A little or a lot    29
Instruction: Learning by association    30
Software Engineering (CASE): Glass box programming    31
Religious Studies: Illuminated scriptures revisited    32
Museum Exhibits: Please touch!    33

## 3    System Design Issues  35

Overview    36
Usability/User Interface: Beyond user-friendly    37
Displays: What you see is what you get    37
Performance: Faster is better    39
Printing: Getting it on paper    39
Versions: Preserving the pattern of changes    40
Networks: Communications across computers    41
Annotation: Users leave their marks    41
Integration: Sharing the wealth    42
Aliasing: Double the meaning, double the fun    43
Fisheye Views: Viewing in context    43
Hierarchical Views: Seeing the forest for the trees    45

## 4    Implementation Issues  47

Overview    48
Navigation: Lost in hyperspace    49
Collaboration: Working together    49
Security: Controlling access    50
Text Conversion: From paper to electrons    51
Compatibility: Every system is an island    52
Rights: Who owns what?    53

Public Access: Power to the people    54
Publishing: Dissemination of hypertext databases    55
Usability Evaluation: Measuring ease of use    56

# 5 Authoring 59

Overview    60
Structuring Hyperknowledge: Exploiting the medium    61
Authoring Principles: The art and the craft    62
Authoring Tools: Hypertext construction sets    63
Screen Formats: Designing the layout    64
Input Modes: Mousing around    65
Graphics: A picture is worth 1K words    67
Sound/Speech: The end of the silent screen    68
Text Editors: Word games    68
Graphics Editors: Making pictures    69
Root Document: It all starts here    71
Document Size: Small is beautiful    71
Cognitive Processes: Links in the mind    72
Electronic Messaging: Telecommunicating    73

# 6 Systems 75

Overview    76
MEMEX: Bush's seminal vision    77
XANADU: Nelson's grand plan    78
AUGMENT: Engelbart makes it work    78
INTERMEDIA: Hypermedia demonstrated    79
NoteCards: Xerox creates an original    82
KMS: The Knowledge Management System    83
Hyperties: The interactive encyclopedia    86
Neptune: Software engineering tool    86
WE: Creative writing environment    88
GUIDE: Hypertext comes to the PC    88
HyperCard: Welcome to the stacks    89
NaviText: Electronic documentation    91
Black Magic: Hypertext word processing    92
askSam: Hypertext database manager    93
KnowledgePro: Hypertext expert system    94

# 7 Personalities 97

Overview  98
Bush  99
Nelson  100
Engelbart  101
Atkinson  101
van Dam  102
Halasz  103
Shneiderman  104

# 8 Possibilities 107

Overview  108
Hyper Travel Guides  109
Hyper Resumes  109
Hyper Job Aids  110
Hyper Blueprints  111
Hyper Magazines  111
Hyper Contracts  113
Hyper Crosswords  113
Hyper Jokes  114
Hyper Cookbooks  114
Hyper Hype?  115

# 9 The End Is Just the Beginning 117

Overview  118
Artificial Intelligence: Making hypertext smarter  119
User Empowerment: Putting users in control  120
The Role of Print: Print versus electronic delivery  121
Business Opportunities: Making hyper bucks  122
Success Factors: Guidelines for managing a hypertext project  124
Getting Started: Your personal odyssey  125

## Appendix/Using the Software Version    127

Overview    127
Using Your Computer    127
Typical Computer Problems and Their Solutions    130
About Hyperties on the IBM PC    132
How to Browse    133
Hyperties Authoring    134


## Bibliography    137

References    137
Hypertext 87 Papers    139
Human Factors Research    144


## Epilog/The Making of *Hypertext Hands-On!*    147

The Development Process    149
What the Reviewers Said    151
Collaboration at a Distance    153
The Only Thing That Doesn't Change Is Change Itself    154


## Hyper Glossary    155


## Index    163

# Introduction

Welcome to *Hypertext Hands-On!* This book explains what hypertext is; the accompanying disk shows you how it works. Together, they should give you a good understanding of why hypertext is such an important and powerful idea.

**Hypertext is usually defined**{3} as the nonlinear viewing of information. "Nonlinear" means that you can examine information in any order you wish by selecting the topic you want to see next. It provides a new way of accessing and organizing any type of information. Hypertext can make it easier and faster to find things and absorb ideas. Instead of having to specify specific keywords or search strings, you simply browse through a **database**{7} by "jumping" from link to link.

Although the content of a hypertext document can be duplicated in print (such as the *Hypertext Hands-On!* book), convenient branching requires a computer system (e.g., an IBM PC and the *Hypertext Hands-On!* disk). In the book, you must look up the linked terms using the page numbers provided; with the disk you simply select the term, press the Enter key, and you can jump directly to the new topic you have selected.

Hypertext as an idea has been around for quite a while. **Vannevar Bush**{99} first suggested the general concept of hypertext in 1945. The term "hypertext" has been popularized by **Ted Nelson**{100} in his many talks and writings. The first hypertext system to be implemented was NLS (now called **Augment**{78}) during the 1960s. In the next two decades, many hypertext systems were created, eventually leading to widely available systems such as **HyperCard**{89} from Apple Computer. The hypertext system used for the *Hypertext Hands-On!* disk, **Hyperties**{86}, was developed at the University of Maryland Human–Computer Interaction Laboratory and is distributed by Cognetics Corporation.

Hypertext has many potential **applications**{20} that are just beginning to be explored: encyclopedias, medical textbooks, technical documentation, instructional materials, and product catalogs. The use of hypertext is also being examined in specialized areas such as dictionaries, creative writing, online help systems, computer-aided software engineering (CASE), religious studies, and museum exhibits. There are many other **hypertext possibilities**{108}, including travel guides, resumes, blueprints, magazines, job aids, contracts, cookbooks, crossword puzzles, and maybe even jokes.

Although hypertext systems have been studied for more than two decades, there are still many issues that are not well understood and are the subject of current research. Some of the **system design issues**{31} include annotation, display capabilities, versioning, integration, performance, printing, networking, and usability. **Implementation issues**{41} that are the subject of much debate include navigation, collaboration, rights, public access, security, compatibility, text conversion, and publishing procedures. New ideas in computer science such as **aliasing**{43} and **fisheye views**{43}, as well as research on the **cognitive processes**{72} underlying hypertext are also being studied.

Hypertext has three important aspects that we are not able to demonstrate fully with the *Hypertext Hands-On!* disk: hypermedia, collaboration, and authoring. *Hypermedia* refers to the capability to create hypertext databases containing a mixture of many different kinds of media, including text, graphics, photographs, video sequences, sound, and voice. To do this, a large capacity, multimedia storage device such as **CD-ROM**{15} is needed.

**Collaboration**{49} refers to the idea that people can interact while creating and reading hypertext documents. On a **networked**{41} system, it is possible for people to share the same documents. In fact this is one of the essential ideas of hypertext—that a distributed database of information can be accessed and added to by many people.

**Authoring**{60} is the term used to describe the creation of hypertext databases. There are a number of authoring principles to be followed in organizing documents and deciding how to link them together. Decisions must also be made about the structuring of knowledge, screen formats, input modes, use of graphics or sound/speech, and document size. A variety of software tools can be used in the authoring process including text editors and graphic editors.

There are many new horizons ahead for hypertext. By applying ideas from **artificial intelligence**{119}, hypertext databases could become far more powerful. By making access to databases and applications programs easier, hypertext may **empower users**{120} more than existing software environments. Hypertext will undoubtedly create many new **business opportunities**{122} ranging from the development of databases to the design of networks.

We think *Hypertext Hands-On!* will provide you with a good introduction to a fascinating topic. The book is organized into the following chapters:

1. Essential Concepts—the major concepts underlying hypertext

2. Applications—the applications currently being explored

3. System Design Issues—features of hypertext systems

4. Implementation Issues—considerations associated with actual use

5. Authoring—creating hypertext documents and databases

6. Systems—describes some of the major hypertext systems

7. Personalities—who's who in the hypertext world

8. Possibilities—future applications of hypertext systems

9. The End Is Just the Beginning—next steps for hypertext

   Appendix/Using the Software Version—how to use Hyperties and the *Hands-On* disk

   Bibliography—references and sources of further information

   Epilog—the development of *Hypertext Hands-On!*

   Glossary—definitions of hypertext terms

Each article in a chapter is self-contained to facilitate **browsing**{10}. Although you can go through the book and disk in a linear fashion, it is assumed that you will want to skip around; *Hypertext Hands-On!* is designed for this style of reading. To learn how to use the *Hypertext Hands-On!* disk, see the appendix.

For other introductory articles about hypertext, see Ambron and Hooper (1988), Conklin (1987), and Yankelovich, Meyrowitz and van Dam (1985) in the **References**{137} section of the Bibliography.

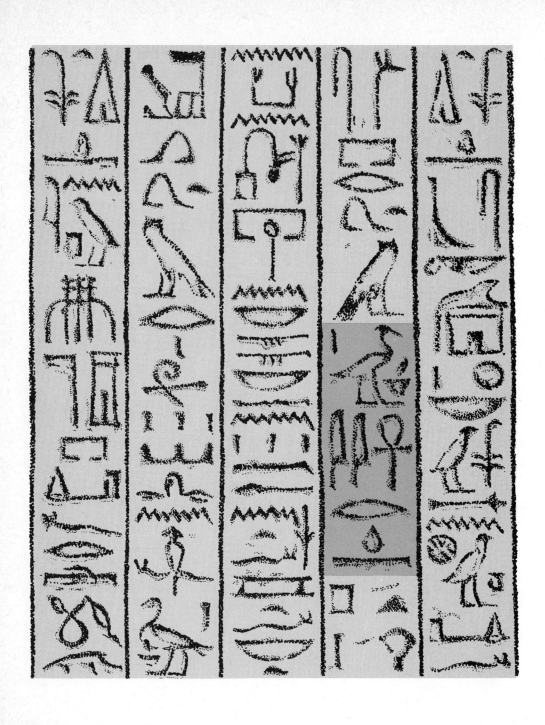

# Essential Concepts

## OVERVIEW

What is hypertext? Hypertext is freedom! Freedom from the burdens of traditional computing applications. Freedom from fear of failure. Every hypertext user succeeds in getting somewhere and getting something. As a hypertext user you are also free to be creative. You can uncover relationships that were not noticed by anyone else. You can read about things that you didn't anticipate finding. The joy of serendipity in reading about something novel and the opportunity for incidental learning while trying to locate a specific fact make hypertext a satisfying adventure for many people who otherwise shun computers.

This chapter introduces you to the essential concepts of hypertext, including the structural elements: **links**{3}, **nodes**{5}, **hierarchies**{6}, and **databases**{7}, as well as how documents are accessed: **windows**{9}, **direct manipulation**{11}, **indexing**{11}, **searching**{12}, **filters**{13}, **tours**{14}, **bookmarks**{14} and **path history**{15}. The significance of **CD-ROM**{15} to hypertext is also discussed.

Wherever possible we have indicated which hypertext systems illustrate specific concepts. The systems are described in Chapter 6.

# DEFINITIONS: Hypertext terminology unraveled

The most common meaning of "hypertext" is a **database**{7} that has active cross-references and allows the reader to "jump" to other parts of the database as desired. This makes the reading (and writing) process nonsequential. It is the requirement for active cross-references that makes a computer necessary to implement hypertext. In this book, we can describe hypertext; however, you must use the software component to experience it.

A hypertext database can be conceptualized as a network of **nodes**{5} and links where documents are the nodes and the links are cross-references. Hypertext networks can take the form of **hierarchies**{6}, but usually the associations among documents are more complex.

The documents linked together are not restricted to text only but could be graphics, photographs, sounds, narration (speech), or animated sequences (video). When the documents are multimedia in nature, the term *hypermedia* is often used. **CD-ROM**{15} is a multimedia storage medium that is likely to become popular for hypermedia applications.

Another important concept of hypertext is the idea that articles are shared across multiple locations/machines and allow **collaboration**{49} in both reading and writing articles. By allowing such connections, it becomes possible for an individual to access a tremendous amount of information. In fact, some hypertext visionaries such as **Vannevar Bush**{99} and **Ted Nelson**{100} have envisioned "giant brains" and "universal databases" in which everything is connected to everything else.

# LINKS: The glue that holds hypertext together

The single most important concept in hypertext is the link. Links are the labels that connect one **node**{5} (document, article, topic) with another. When a link is activated (e.g., by selecting it with a mouse or arrow keys), a jump is made to the document the link points to. The link may be embedded in the body of the document, embedded as part of a graphic or video image, listed at the end of the document, or contained in an index.

Links are usually denoted by words or phrases that are highlighted in some fashion, but they can also be **graphics**{67} or *icons*. For example, each component of a schematic diagram may be a link to a more detailed schematic of that component or to a text description. Links can produce a variety of different results. They can:

- transfer to a new topic

- show a reference (or go from a reference to the article)

- provide ancillary information, such as a footnote, definition, or annotation

- display an illustration, schematic, photograph, or video sequence

- display an index

- run another program (e.g., a spreadsheet or animation)

A hypertext system may have only one type of link or many types. In some systems, the user may be able to select which link types are active. When a user selects a link, the display of the new node may replace the original node, or it may share the display via an overlapping **window**{9}. In some systems, the user can partition the screen in separate windows where different nodes are displayed.

Links can be unidirectional or bidirectional. A unidirectional link goes in one direction only; a bidirectional link goes in both directions. A bidirectional link allows you to traverse the link from either end. Links are usually given names that may or may not be shown to the user. The link name can indicate the two nodes it connects and its type. For example, a bidirectional link that connects node 54 with reference 23 might be named n54r23bi.

Links can also be hierarchical or nonhierarchical in their organization. In a hierarchical system, all nodes are arranged in a tree structure and each node must be traced through this structure. **Hierarchical**{6} structures allow documents to be organized and searched in a well-prescribed manner; that is, each level of the hierarchy provides more detail or certain types of information.

Links must be easy to activate (typically a single "point and select" action) and must produce fast response. If links are cumbersome to activate or slow to produce results, people tend to use them infrequently, minimizing the main value of hypertext (see **performance**{39}). Creating and updating links represents one of the major tasks in **authoring**{60} a hypertext document. The author must choose labels for the links that easily identify their referents. **Authoring tools**{63} for hypertext systems must provide the capabilities to add, delete, modify, list, and define the types of links.

One of the major controversies surrounding links is "granularity;" that is, whether a link points only to the beginning of another document or to an interior paragraph, sentence, or word. Proponents of simplicity argue for links to documents only, whereas devotees of precision and detail argue for within-document links.

## NODES: Units of information

A single document in a hypertext database is called a node. Each node in a hypertext system corresponds to one or more screen displays. Nodes are called frames (**KMS**{83}), statements (**Augment**{78}), articles (**Hyperties**{86}), and cards (**NoteCard**{82}, **HyperCard**{89}) in different systems. Although there is no generally accepted guideline for **document size**{71}, a document usually describes a single concept or topic. Hypertext documents are usually written so that they are self-contained and do not depend upon the user's having viewed other documents. Continuity between documents is provided by links.

Some hypertext systems allow nodes to be different types (e.g., references, annotations, illustrations, etc.). Typed nodes are usually identified by different colors, fonts, or icons when viewed by the user. For example, in the **GUIDE**{88} system, the cursor icon changes from an arrow to a rectangle to an asterisk to denote elaborations, new documents, and pop-up notes. Some hypertext systems require nodes to have titles. This is an extra burden for the author, but it seems to reduce disorientation significantly.

Nodes can also be composites, that is, several nodes linked together and referenced by a single name. This is useful if the author or user wants to have a series of documents displayed in sequential order (but still be accessed as individual nodes). The **Intermedia**{79} system provides this capability via *webs*.

Because of the modularity inherent in hypertext documents, they are not well suited to information that has a strong sequential nature (such as traditional prose or poetry). On the other hand, for information that has a richer network organization (such as reference books, texts, guidelines, catalogs, and technical manuals), hypertext provides many advantages over traditional linear formats. Furthermore, hypertext opens up new possibilities for existing literature, such as interactive fiction where the reader controls the plot development (see **creative writing**{27}).

Node size is a regular topic of debate in the hypertext community. Some advocate small nodes, the size of one screen; others argue that larger nodes reduce disorientation and enable authors to segment the material as they see fit. Excess fragmentation can be confusing, whereas insufficient modularization can produce too much annoying page turning on small computer screens.

## HIERARCHIES: Structuring the nodes and links

The structure of a hypertext database is a major factor that determines how easy it is to create, use, and update. One way of organizing a hypertext database that simplifies **browsing**{10} and **authoring**{60} is a hierarchical structure.

In a hierarchy, each node has a parent (superordinate concept) and a child (subordinate concept) unless the node is a starting point (root) or an end point (leaf). A hypertext database organized as a hierarchy can be drawn as a tree structure with no cross-over links. A hypertext database that allows multiple links between parent and child nodes is not a strict hierarchy but a network (see Figure 1.1).

The advantage of a hierarchical structure is that all links must follow an orderly route through the tree, connecting superordinate and subordinate nodes. A **browser**{10} can show the structure of the database as a tree diagram. Because the structure of the database is well defined, various display techniques (such as **fisheye**{43} or **hierarchical views**{45}) can be applied.

The disadvantage of a hierarchical structure is that the flexibility of the links among nodes is limited. All nodes must be linked together via some super/subordinate concepts, not in an arbitrary manner. Being able to link any pair of nodes results in a much richer network of relationships—albeit more difficult to create, use, and maintain.

## DATABASES: Getting organized

Computerized databases emerged in the 1950s but it took until the 1970s before there were widely available database management systems that provided formal data models, data definition languages, sophisticated data manipulation languages, and simple query facilities. Relational and bibliographic database systems have come to be a major computing application on all types of systems.

The relational data model and its variants are used in popular personal computer programs such as *dBase III*, *Rbase*, and *Paradox*. Mainframe systems include IBM's DB2 with the SQL language, and minicomputer

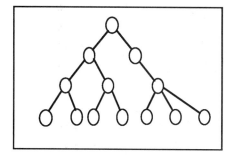 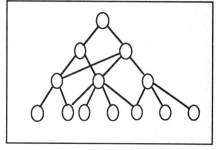

**Figure 1.1**　Hierarchical tree structure (left) and network structure (right).

systems include INGRES from *Relational Technology, Inc.* The relational data model is based on a tabular representation, with rows and columns of data. Each row is unique, and each item in a row is atomic (cannot be broken down into smaller pieces). Users can select rows or columns, sort or group related rows, and join one table to another based on common values.

The relational data model is great for business data, some scientific databases, and situations that have neatly structured fields of information. The network or hierarchical data models are two other effective methods for dealing with structured data. However, if the data is largely texts, graphics (e.g., weather maps, schematics), images (e.g., X-rays, photos), or sounds, then these data models and database management systems are less effective.

A second major category of databases are organized around the principles of bibliographic information retrieval systems. The Library of Congress has almost six million card catalog records available for search through the SCORPIO system. Users can type an author's name, a book title, or a subject and get back a set of catalog records. Users can combine terms with ANDs and ORs to refine their queries (this more elaborate approach is called Boolean **searching**{12} after the mathematician George Boole). The Lockheed DIALOG system provides access to almost 200 million abstracts of articles from scientific journals. Other services provide access to millions of legal citations, magazine articles, the New York Times articles, the Associate Press and United Press International news reports, and stock market evaluations. Some information retrieval systems, such as the one for the U.S. Patent Office, enable users to retrieve pictures based on keyword searches.

Both the structured data models and the information retrieval approach become less effective if the data has a more complex organization. Hypertext systems can help in dealing with richly structured or interconnected data items that come from textual, graphic, or audio sources. A hypertext database supports structured and arbitrary links among materials that are contained in a node. Since the node can be large, it may contain an entire picture, speech, song, article, legal decision, or biography and can be easily linked to related nodes. Hypertext databases can be vast, can include multimedia sources (audio, videodisc, CD-ROM, etc.), and can enable exploratory browsing. Of course, the increased flexibility of hypertext databases leads to a greater chance of disorientation (see **navigation**{49}).

## WINDOWS: Multiple views

Organizing information on a computer screen so that it is easily understandable is a significant challenge. One technique that usually improves readability and comprehension is to partition the screen in two or more separate viewing areas called windows. Different parts of a document or different application programs can be viewed simultaneously. Studies by Tombaugh, Wright, and Lickorish at Cambridge University have shown the advantage of multiple windows in text reading tasks.

Window sizes and locations on the screen may be fixed by the designer or changed by the user. Windows may overlap each other or they may partition the screen into sections called *tiling*. Experienced computer users often prefer to change window sizes and location in an over-lapped layout called the "cluttered desktop model." However, for many users this increases the cognitive load and leads to confusion. A well designed tiled layout with fixed sizes and location suited to the user's tasks may be more effective in many situations. A 1986 study at Xerox's Palo Alto Research Center by S. Bly and J. Rosenberg found support for the effectiveness of each strategy in differing situations.

Multiple windows are an important part of **NoteCards**{82}, which was designed to facilitate information integration from multiple sources during creative authoring sessions. On the other hand, **browsing**{10} software for novice users at a museum exhibit might be easiest to use if there is only a single window.

Information inside windows may scroll up automatically or the user may control the scrolling by pressing a key or a scroll bar (e.g., **GUIDE**{88}). In some systems, information does not scroll but is paged—each display is a separate page (as in **Hyperties**{86}). In systems where users have control over the windows, a window is typically activated or opened by selecting some action or command. The window is deactivated or closed by another action or command.

Determining suitable **screen formats**{64} is a major step in the authoring process. Windowing capability can make this step easier because a lot of the display layout is handled automatically or can be determined by the user.

For further discussions of windows, see Tombaugh et al. (1987) and Bly and Rosenberg (1986) in the **References**{137}.

## BROWSING: Exploring a hypertext system

Hypertext systems offer a surprising and satisfying freedom to explore. With little training in computer concepts and with little knowledge of the subject domain, hypertext users can casually traverse nodes and links looking for something of interest. **Direct manipulation**{11} enables an easy-to-use mode of interaction; reversibility of action conveys a sense of safety and security.

This is in contrast to most existing database systems, which access carefully structured data records based on part numbers, catalog numbers, specified keywords, individual names, or other identifiers. Conventional database systems require users to learn a complex query language and to master computer concepts of the relational data model or boolean expressions (terms combined with ANDs and ORs).

However, there is a dark side to the force! The freedom to explore can be a distraction from the intended goal of answering a specific fact-oriented question. The ease of traversal can quickly lead you into the lost regions of hyperspace where disorientation sets in and **navigation**{49} becomes difficult. Careful design of the browsing software and the database can reduce the problem but hypertext orienteering can still be a challenge.

For further discussion of the difference between browsing in a hypertext system and searching in a database system, see Marchionini and Shneiderman (1988) in the **References**{137}.

## DIRECT MANIPULATION: See and point interfaces

Early software designers created command languages because they had to assume a teletype keyboard and slow displays. Now with pointing devices such as the mouse or touch screen and large high-speed displays, new opportunities are available. Instead of typing, users can point at visual displays of the objects and actions of interest and immediately see the results of their selections. This interaction style with rapid, incremental, and reversible actions has been termed direct manipulation, because the user appears to be dealing directly with visible representations of the objects and actions in the real world.

WYSIWYG (What You See Is What You Get) display editors, spreadsheets, many videogames, and the Macintosh desktop are frequently cited examples of direct manipulation interfaces. In most hypertext systems, you move a cursor to a highlighted term or graphic component. Then you simply click, touch, or press to follow a link to another node. This form of direct manipulation simplifies learning and enables rapid traversal with low error rates. Reversibility is usually provided. In many hypertext systems users can also select by pointing at a textual or graphic index. This simple approach enables you to concentrate on the contents. Because the distraction of dealing with complex commands is eliminated, you can focus on the task, and the computer becomes transparent.

For further discussion of direct manipulation, see Shneiderman (1983) in the **References**{137}.

## INDEXING: Making order of the chaos

Although links provide the primary means of connecting information in hypertext systems, an important secondary capability is indexing. Indexing makes it possible to look up information alphabetically or to search for specific terms. Information can also be indexed **hierarchically**{6} in a table of contents or outline that matches the structure of the hypertext documents.

An alphabetical list of article titles (as in the **Hyperties**{86} INDEX) can be useful in trying to locate information about a major concept known to the reader. However, there may be terms used in an article that are not included in an article title. This problem can be resolved by an alphabetical term list with pointers to the related articles (similar to an index with page numbers at the back of a printed book).

Another possibility is to have a table of contents that lists the article titles in meaningful groups, in meaningful orders, like the print version of *Hypertext Hands-On!*. In fact, the nonlinearity of hypertext documents allows several tables of contents portraying alternate organizations.

A comprehensive word index in which every word (except for frequent words such as ''the'') appears is sometimes used as an index. This approach, called a concordance, assures comprehensive access but consumes large amounts of storage, can be overwhelming, and is tedious to browse.

A serious limitation of indexing is that the author may not have indexed the particular word or phrase that the reader wants to locate. Therefore most hypertext systems provide a text-searching capability.

## SEARCHING: Finding something

Although **browsing**{10} provides one means of finding things in a hypertext database, it works only for predefined links. A more general capability is keyword search that finds a word or phrase provided as input. Almost all database systems (as well as word processing programs) provide some form of keyword or text string search capability.

There are a number of desirable features in a search function. This includes the ability to specify case-sensitivity (i.e., whether to ignore upper/lower case), boolean expressions (terms combined with AND, OR, NOT), and ''wild card'' characters that do not have to be matched.

Hypertext systems are often confused with text search systems that find keywords in context. Such ''brute force'' search methods are relatively easy to implement but are only partially successful because it is difficult for the user to determine which of the ''hits'' are relevant.

The process is like trying to read a book from the index. You may be catapulted into the middle of a database and may become disoriented.

Search algorithms are useful in some database situations but can distract readers from making a serious effort to understand the structure and contents of a database. They are most valuable when the query is of the form: "Does this keyword exist literally in the database?" Their value decreases when common words that occur frequently are used in the search.

Searching capabilities are becoming increasingly common in hypertext systems. The Washington University **Medical Handbook**{23} and the **NAVITEXT**{91} systems include examples of search capability. A distinction should be made between systems that support search within a node and those that search the entire database; these are different capabilities.

## FILTERS: Narrowing the search

Limiting the information displayed in a meaningful way is important in any large hypertext system. For example, you may want to see only recent information or information that pertains to one subject area. Filters are the mechanism provided in many hypertext systems to provide this kind of selectivity.

Filters can be implemented via keywords; only the documents containing the specified keywords would be displayed. Filtering can also be accomplished by specifying the attributes of nodes or links (e.g., creation date, author) to be displayed or not displayed. For example, a user could specify that no reference links be shown or that links to summary documents only are to be displayed. Another filter might be to locate all nodes within three jumps from the current node.

Filtering and search capabilities should be complementary. The purpose of a filter is to restrict the amount of information displayed; the role of searching capabilities is to locate specific information.

## TOURS: Down the yellow brick path

Although the fundamental concept of hypertext is to let you choose your own path through a nonlinear database, in some contexts (e.g., a tutorial or an orientation) it is desirable to create a prespecified path. This is called a tour.

In a tour, all link selections are done automatically and the system runs by itself. A tour is usually accompanied by commentary that explains what is happening. The commentary may appear in a **window**{9}, or it may be spoken narrative.

A tour provides a *default* path, but readers should be able to interrupt the tour to review a previous screen or simply to pause. There also should be an exit option to quit the tour at any time.

In a way, you could consider the printed version of *Hypertext Hands-On!* to be a tour of the disk version. It is basically the same content but organized in a sequential and structured form. In other words, tours become the metaphor for a linear version of hypertext databases.

## BOOKMARKS: Electronic placemarkers

When reading a hypertext document, you may want to mark a specific location to find it easily later. This marking capability is called bookmarking and is analogous to marking a page in a book.

A bookmark is usually created by a command or by pressing a special key. In some systems, the bookmark can be given a name as a memory aid. When the bookmark is activated, the system displays the marked page. Bookmarks are often used to mark restart points when reading is interrupted. When you restart the hypertext system, you can automatically return to the marked locations if you choose.

# PATH HISTORY: Keeping track and going back

Many hypertext systems provide for reversibility; that is, you can re-trace your steps and return to previous screens or articles. This possibility is important for a sense of safety and to provide a lucid model of traversal so as to reduce disorientation (see **navigation**{49}). A path history capability allows the user and system to keep track of previous documents viewed.

**Hyperties**{86} supports reversibility with the RETURN TO command on the bottom of each screen. This feature enables the user to back up one article at a time all the way to the beginning. Hyperties also has a HISTORY feature, which displays a list of all articles read in a session.

**HyperCard**{89} offers a menu item called Recent that shows postage stamp-sized images of the 42 most recently visited cards. If you recognize the card you want to go back to, you can jump there with one simple mouse click.

# CD-ROM: Storage for the masses

*Hypermedia* refers to the idea of organizing different media (text, graphics, audio, video) in a hypertext format. This introduces the need for a high-capacity, fast-access digital storage method. Laser optical disk technology meets this need. Compact disks (CDs) provide a compact form of digital storage with tremendous capacity and rapid access.

CDs are 12 cm in diameter and hold approximately 600 *megabytes* of information (equivalent to about 150,000 typed pages). All information stored on CDs is in digital form, including text, photographs, audio, and video. Because CDs are read by a laser beam and involve no contact, they should never wear out, regardless of the number of accesses made.

CD-ROM refers to the form of CD technology intended to be used as a read-only storage device for computers. The media format is defined technically in a specification published by Philips and Sony. A number of companies make CD-ROM players for personal computers. In 1986, a newer standard called CD-Interactive (CD-I) was agreed upon by Philips, Sony, and other consumer/computer electronics companies. The CD-I format involves the same 12-cm disk but includes programs encoded on the disk that can be read via an appropriate interface. With CD-ROM formats, the computer program must control the disk; CD-I format allows the disk to contain control programs itself.

A number of companies have released information in CD format to be used with CD-ROM technology. Grolier Electronic Publishing sells its electronic **encyclopedia**{22} on CD and Microsoft markets the "Bookshelf" CD that includes Roget's Thesaurus, Bartlett's Quotations, and the World Almanac. Dialog Information Systems now provides portions of its online databases in CD-ROM form. Many publishing companies have announced their intention to market CD-I disks and are likely to use hypermedia techniques.

See Lambert and Ropiequet (1986) in the **References**{137}.

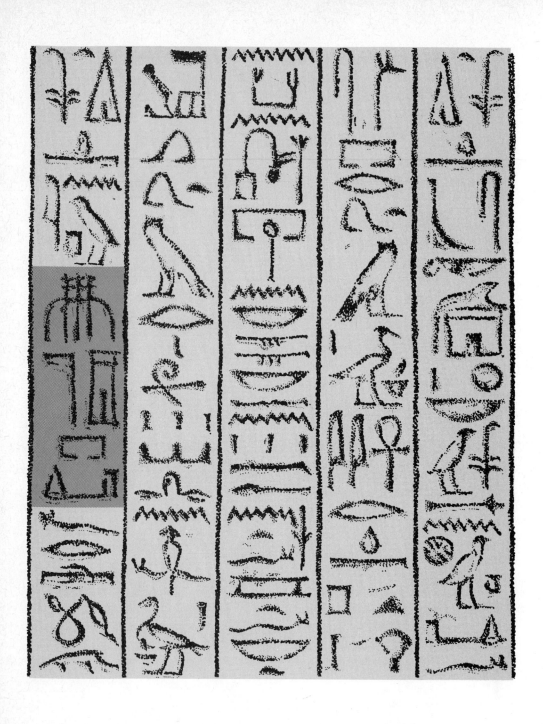

# 2

# Applications

## OVERVIEW

In order to understand what hypertext is, it is important to understand how it can be used. This chapter examines a number of hypertext application areas currently being investigated, including **dictionaries**{21}, **encyclopedias**{22}, **medical textbooks**{23}, **product catalogs**{25}, **creative writing**{27}, **help systems**{28}, **technical documentation**{29}, **instruction**{30}, **software engineering (CASE)** {31}, **religious studies**{32}, and **museum exhibits**{33}. Examples of hypertext systems designed for each of these areas are discussed. Chapter 8 discusses additional possibilities for hypertext applications.

# DICTIONARIES: Lexicographical links

Dictionaries and other writer's tools such as thesauri, books of quotations, and style guides are good candidates for hypertext because of the many cross-references in such works.

Consider the *Oxford English Dictionary* (OED) as an example. The *OED* is the largest dictionary of English consisting of 12 books containing references to over 42 million words. The text of the *OED* already exists in electronic form and could be designed as a hypertext database for its next edition.

The primary benefit of having the *OED* in hypertext form is to support **browsing**{10}. Hypertext would allow readers to follow their own interests when studying entries. In a dictionary the size of the *OED*, hypertext should make it much easier and faster to get from one entry to another.

Creating a hypertext version of the *OED* involves a tremendous **text conversion**{51} project. Links must be identified and coded in each entry. Cross-references represent the most obvious source of links. The *OED* contains 475,000 cross-references for an average of 1.88 links per entry. Lexicographical references (derivations of a word) are another likely source of links. However, these links will involve a lot more effort to identify because the root may not be in the appropriate form for every derivative word.

Additional capabilities that users would want in a hypertext dictionary include the ability to formulate search requests (e.g., "Find all derivations of the current word that originated from Latin"), create **annotations**{41} and **bookmarks**{14}, and cut and paste entries into other documents or programs. Some users might like to have entries or links pronounced via **speech**{68} synthesis. Illustrated dictionaries would involve **graphics**{67}.

You may want to create a dictionary or glossary for a specialized field that interests you. Whether you deal with woodworking, antitrust laws, or recombinant DNA, you could create a useful educational tool for novices in your field of expertise (see **getting started**{125}).

For more on hypertext and the *OED*, see the article by Raymond and Tompa, in **Hypertext 87 Papers**{139} and in the **References**{137}.

## ENCYCLOPEDIAS: Linking up knowledge

Hypertext addresses some of the weaknesses of print encyclopedias. Most encyclopedia entries have extensive cross-references to other entries. Instead of just listing cross-references at the end of the entry, hypertext allows them to be active links that automatically jump to the other articles.

Another weakness of print encyclopedias is the difficulty of finding something. Encyclopedias feature comprehensive indexes, but you have to know (or discover from cross-references) what index term to use. In a hypertext encyclopedia, you can use related terms to find quickly what you are looking for. In addition, some hypertext systems feature **search**{12} capabilities that allow you to enter your own keywords or terms.

One potential advantage of using hypertext for encyclopedias is that it eliminates the shelf space and inconvenience associated with large, heavy books. For example, the print version of the Grolier *Encyclopedia* encompasses 20 thick volumes; the CD version takes up less than ⅓ of the disk including 50 megabytes of indexes. Hypermedia and the use of **CD-ROM**{15} make it possible to include a wider variety of information in an encyclopedia including audio and video sequences, photographs, and drawings.

Of course, in order to use a hypertext encyclopedia, you need to have access to a suitable computer system. **Public access**{54} to and **publishing**{55} of hypertext databases are important issues related to the availability of encyclopedias in hypertext form.

## MEDICAL TEXTBOOKS: Diagnostic tools

Medical practitioners or researchers must deal with huge amounts of information. To make a correct diagnosis or reach a correct conclusion, it is necessary to cross-check many facts and interpretations. Hypertext may be able to improve the speed and accuracy of medical information management.

The *Dynamic Medical Handbook* project at the Washington University School of Medicine in St. Louis involves the development of their medical therapeutics manual in hypertext form. Figure 2.1 shows a sample of a "card" from the prototype along with links. The first sentence of a card is used as the link name to increase the meaningfulness of the link.

Because the manual is a diagnostic tool, the major focus of the effort lies in discovering the best **indexing**{11} and **searching**{12} mechanisms. The usual method for finding information in a hypertext database is by jumping from node to node via links. In contrast, the usual

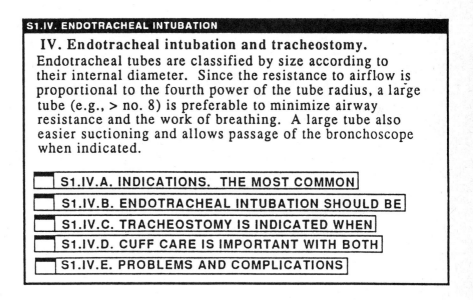

**Figure 2.1**   Sample card from *Dynamic Medical Handbook* (from *Hypertext 87 Proceedings*).

method for searching in information retrieval systems is text string pattern matching.

In the *Dynamic Medical Handbook* project, these two methods have been combined. Each hypertext card has a numerical weight based upon the number of links it has with other cards. When the reader enters a search term, the system retrieves cards in terms of their weights, thus displaying the most "related" links. Figure 2.2 illustrates a search card with weights shown on the left of each link.

Other medical hypertext projects underway include:

- A Drug Information database under development at Johns Hopkins Hospital designed to replace a variety of drug reference books used in hospitals.

- A textbook of internal medicine called the InforMed Project being jointly developed by Columbia-Presbyterian Hospital and BRS Information Technologies. This database will cover five different levels of expertise ranging from patient to subspecialist levels.

- The Explorer-1 knowledge management system developed by Harvard Medical School for the application areas of differential diagnosis, diagnostic work-ups, and medical pathophysiology.

Many medical texts are well suited to hypertext and hypermedia applications. The popular *Physicians Desk Reference* would be a good

```
┌─────────────────────────────────────────────────────────────┐
│ Tracheostomy                                                  │
├─────────────────────────────────────────────────────────────┤
│  (96) ▢ S1.VI.F.2.b. THERAPY SHOULD INCLUDE APPROPRIATE       │
│  (96) ▢ S1.V.G.2.c. IF MANUAL VENTILATION IS DIFFICULT, CHECK │
│  (96) ▢ S1.IV.E.6. EROSION INTO THE INNOMINATE ARTERY WITH    │
│  (96) ▢ S1.IV.E.3. TRACHEOSTOMY TUBE DISLODGEMENT OR CUFF     │
│  (96) ▢ S1.IV.D. CUFF CARE IS IMPORTANT WITH BOTH             │
│  (96) ▢ S1.IV.C. TRACHEOSTOMY IS INDICATED WHEN               │
│ (336) ▢ S1.IV.E. ENDOTRACHEAL INTUBATION AND TRACHEOSTOMY.    │
└─────────────────────────────────────────────────────────────┘
```

**Figure 2.2** Sample search result in the *Dynamic Medical Handbook* (from *Hypertext 87 Proceedings*).

candidate for hypertext because of the many cross-references among diseases, symptoms, drug interactions, and so on. Anatomy and physiology books could take advantage of the capability to link illustrations and photographs or animated sequences to text.

For more on hypertext and medical texts, see the article by Frisse in the **Hypertext 87 Papers**{139} and in the **References**{137}.

## PRODUCT CATALOGS: Let your fingers do the walking

One of the difficulties in designing or using a product catalog is the many different ways that products can be organized (by function, by product codes, by size, by pricing, etc.) Printed catalogs allow only one possible order, although cross-references and multiple indexes can help. However, following multiple page references can be tedious in printed catalogs.

The Savings Zone Club disk is an example of a hypertext product catalog. Developed for the Apple Macintosh using the **GUIDE**{88} system, it provides descriptions of over 700 products sold by the Savings Zone (see Figure 2.3). An interesting aspect of this disk is that it also includes a space adventure game that has product names embedded in the story. The space adventure game also uses hypertext to link **graphics**{67} to text sequences and other graphics (see Figure 2.4).

Some of the potential benefits of using hypertext for presentations of products and services are that

- information on price and availability can be updated easily
- online ordering is possible
- nonlinear presentation may reduce information overload
- cross-referencing to accessories/options is facilitated
- browsing may lead to additional business
- animated demonstrations are possible

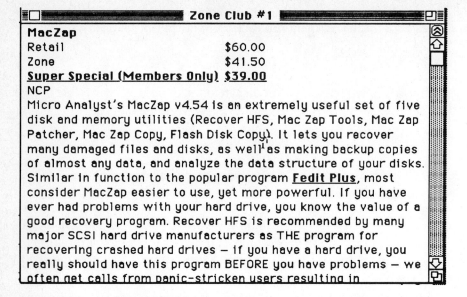

**Figure 2.3**  Example product screen from the Zone Club disk. (Courtesy, the Savings Zone.)

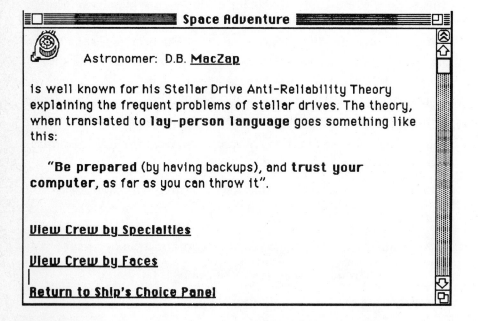

**Figure 2.4**  Space adventure screen with product link on Zone Club disk. (Courtesy, the Savings Zone.)

On the other hand, using hypertext may have the following disadvantages:

- customers must have the appropriate computer

- scope and breadth of offerings may be less evident

- may not have the photographic detail of print catalogs

- online ordering may be more complex than phone or mail orders

Hypertext product catalogs are likely to be most advantageous for product lines that are very large, that change frequently, or that have many interrelated components. Can you imagine getting your next Sears or Neiman-Marcus catalog in hypertext form?

## CREATIVE WRITING: Interactive fiction

Although it is usual to associate hypertext with scholarly and technical writing, it can also be a medium for creative writing. Hypertext makes interactive fiction possible. Instead of a fixed sequence of events, the reader decides what will happen next by choosing to explore certain links. This provides the ultimate in reader involvement because in a very real sense the reader decides how the story develops.

Of course the author still needs to develop plots and outcomes. However, the author of an interactive story writes a series of episodes, each having connections to other episodes. Like any kind of hypertext **authoring**{60}, interactive fiction is more complex than conventional linear writing.

Storyspace is a hypertext system developed at the University of North Carolina to study creative writing. The system provides a special editor for creating stories that depicts the story as a network of units (see Figure 2.5). The story editor makes it easy for the author to indicate links between episodes and to experiment with different story structures.

Will hypertext lead to a new generation of avant-garde writers who go beyond Joyce, Salinger, Pound, Eliot, and Borges? How about hypermedia plays, poems, and movies? Look out Shakespeare and Steven Spielberg!

For further discussion of hypertext and creative writing, see the article by Bolter and Joyce in the **Hypertext 87 Papers**{139}.

## HELP SYSTEMS: Context-sensitive assistance

Almost everyone who uses a computer system eventually encounters situations where they need immediate assistance. Help systems are intended to provide information that will allow you to continue with your task. Most help systems simply act as online reference manuals and show the user an explanation of a command or result. Some help systems provide context-sensitive information, that is, advice that is specific to the currently active function. A few help systems provide multiple levels or types of explanation.

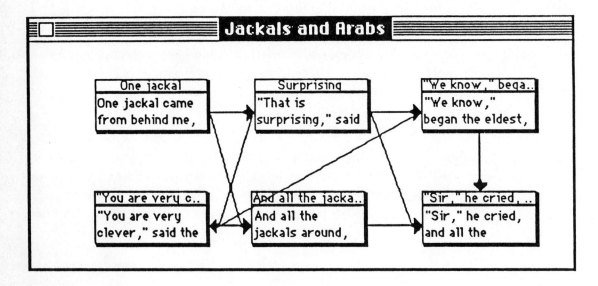

**Figure 2.5**  Storyspace editor screen. (From *Hypertext 87 Proceedings*.)

Hypertext can be used to develop a help system with a high degree of context sensitivity. Menu options or field names can link to an explanation of their function. **Browsing**{10} capability can be used to help the user find program functions or data. One of the advantages of using hypertext to create a help system is that it can make help easily available but also can be unobtrusive. Many of the hypertext systems available for personal computers, such as **HyperCard**{89}, **GUIDE**{88}, and **askSam**{93}, feature context-sensitive help systems.

For more information about online help systems, see Kearsley (1988) in the **References**{137}.

## TECHNICAL DOCUMENTATION: A little or a lot

Almost all products and computer programs of any complexity involve a variety of technical documentation — reference guides, operating manuals, and tutorials. One benefit of using hypertext for documentation is that the relationships between ideas can be seen easily. Another benefit is that hypertext can reduce the size of documentation. It is not uncommon for complicated systems or equipment to have thousands of pages of printed documentation, only a small portion of which is needed at any one time. Hypertext can store information until it is needed. Imagine the benefits of reducing the 150 pounds of paper documentation carried on the NASA space shuttle or the 41,000 pounds carried on a U.S. Navy destroyer.

An example of hypertext documentation is the Document Examiner program marketed by Symbolics, Inc., for its AI work stations. The program allows users to learn about the Symbolics system by searching through topics, specifying keywords, or **browsing**{10} through the content. The Document Examiner also allows **bookmarks**{14}, and **annotation**{41}.

An experimental hypertext system called Thoth II was used to create a VW hypermanual, a repair manual for the VW Rabbit. Nodes correspond to parts of the car, status of the parts, or symptoms. Links define how parts work together (e.g., the fuel system), principles of operation (e.g., combustion), or causes of failures (e.g., clogged fuel filters). In this kind of hypertext documentation, **graphics**{67} links are very important. Hypertext is especially well suited to the diagnostic repair aspect of technical documentation (see **job aids**{110}).

For more about hypertext and documentation, see the articles by Walker on the Document Examiner system and Collier on Thoth II in the **Hypertext 87 Papers**{139}.

## INSTRUCTION: Learning by association

Computers have been used in education for many years with mixed results. Hypertext may offer a highly effective learning medium. To the extent that hypertext emphasizes the relationships between concepts in a subject domain, it may make the subject easier to learn (see **cognitive processes**{72}). A number of interesting projects are being conducted to explore the potential of hypertext for education.

The CSILE project at the University of Toronto uses hypertext to encourage learning among elementary and secondary students via shared databases. One of the major goals of the project is to foster higher order learning strategies in acquiring, organizing, evaluating, and communicating knowledge.

The Palenque project at the Bank Street College in New York is concerned with exploring hypermedia for teaching young children. Palenque is a multimedia database about an ancient Mayan site in the Yucatan Peninsula. It facilitates open-ended exploration and discovery. Children are provided with a "camera" tool that lets them store items of interest and build their own "album" of their trip.

The Perseus project at Harvard University is attempting to develop a hypermedia database about classical Greece that will contain over 100 megabytes of textual information and 10,000 images on **CD-ROM**{15}. The material is to be used in courses on Greek civilization and art as well as by classics scholars. An important consideration in this database is the capability to search information using standard classic citations (e.g., Herodotus 7.132).

As for the effects of hypertext in teaching, there is some evidence from evaluation of the **Intermedia**{79} system that it can result in a deeper understanding of the material taught. In an English class at Brown in which Intermedia was used, students asked more questions and made more observations than those in classes that did not use the system. Students who used Intermedia in a biology course reported learning more than students who took the same course without the system.

Hypertext may not be appropriate in some cases for instruction if the learner needs to follow a step-by-step learning sequence. However, through the use of **tours**{14}, it is possible to use a hypertext database in a linear fashion.

See the articles by Crane on the Perseus project and by Beeman et al. on the use of Intermedia in the **Hypertext 87 Papers**{139}.

## SOFTWARE ENGINEERING (CASE): Glass box programming

The development of a computer system involves many different kinds of documents, including specifications, user and program documentation, source and object code listings, test plans and results, and troubleshooting logs. Managing all of these documents in a large project and keeping them up to date is a major undertaking.

Keeping all information as a hypertext database could have many advantages. The most important benefit is the ability to link all documents referring to the same function so that changes are made simultaneously in each document. For example, if a change is made to a print routine in the source code, the system can identify where this routine is referenced in the documentation, test plan, specifications, and so on. Another important feature is multiple **windows**{9} that allow programmers to see different parts of a program or program and documentation simultaneously. Because of the explicit links in a program (to program subroutines and variables), hypertext appears to be ideally suited.

DynamicDesign is a Computer Aided Software Engineering (CASE) system developed for the C programming language using the **Neptune**{86} hypertext system. The different categories of information that are interconnected via hypertext in DynamicDesign include documentation, specifications, source and object code, implementation notes, symbol tables, and project status. A very important capability provided in DynamicDesign is that it can keep track of different **versions**{40} of the program under development.

For more information on the DynamicDesign system, see the article by Bigelow and Riley in the **Hypertext 87 Papers**{139}.

## RELIGIOUS STUDIES: Illuminated scriptures revisited

Religious scholars all over the world spend a good deal of time analyzing passages in the Bible, Talmud, Koran, Book of Mormon, and other religious works. Hypertext versions of these books would make it possible to explicitly show the relationships among ideas, and to link original texts to multiple commentaries.

AIRS, Inc., is currently developing a hypertext system using CD-ROM called The Bible Library. It consists of four translations of the Bible and twelve related works, including a Bible dictionary and encyclopedia. Users of The Bible Library will be able to browse an index of every word in the Bible as well as to compare information in side-by-side windows.

There is some irony in the use of hypertext for religious documents because both writing and printing were fostered by the desire to record religious tracts. Furthermore, the illuminated manuscripts originally penned by monks often had copious margin notes and footnotes to explain the main text. One could view the use of hypertext for religious documents as the continuation of a very old tradition.

# MUSEUM EXHIBITS: Please touch!

Hypertext can add new dimensions to museum exhibits and provide visitors with a greater degree of involvement. Through the use of hypermedia, it would be possible for even small museums to have a large database of multimedia information available. Furthermore, hypertext databases allow museum visitors to select information of personal interest to themselves.

For example, **Hyperties**{86} has been used in an exhibit of the photographs of David Seymour at galleries in Washington, D.C., and New York City. In March 1988, a Hyperties system using a touch screen was installed at the Smithsonian Museum of Natural History for an exhibit called "King Herod's Dream." The exhibit deals with the rise of urbanism and archaeological methods at the Roman port city of Caesarea. The database offered visitors information on joining one of 200 archaeological digs during the coming year. The database was updated for showings at the Los Angeles County Art Museum and then for showings in Denver, Minneapolis, Boston, and Ottawa. Hyperties will also be used for a multimedia **encyclopedia**{22} containing 3000 articles and 10,000 videodisk images about the Holocaust being prepared for the Museum of Jewish Heritage in New York City.

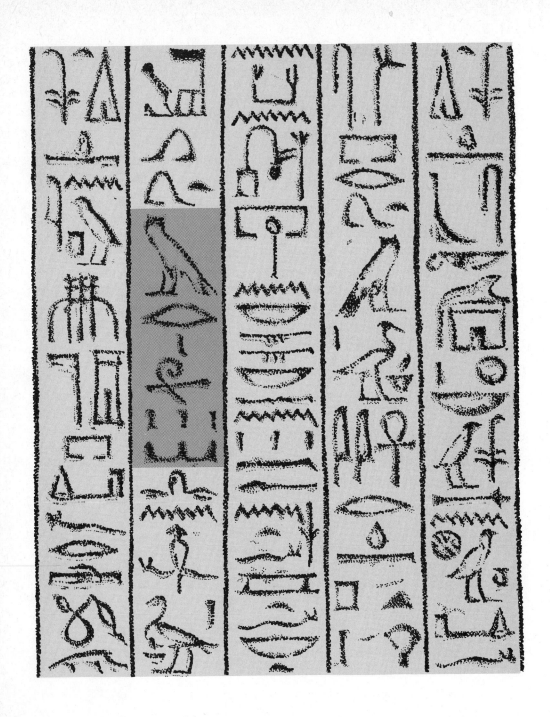

# System Design Issues

**3**

## OVERVIEW

This chapter discusses current issues in the design of hypertext systems, including **usability**{37}, **displays**{37}, **performance**{39}, **printing-**{39}, **versions**{40}, **networking**{41}, **annotation**{41}, **integration**{42}, **aliasing**{43}, **fisheye views**{43}, and **hierarchical views**{45}. Issues pertaining to the implementation of hypertext systems are discussed in Chapter 4. Note that it is our intent only to identify these issues, not to provide in-depth analyses or attempt solutions.

The decisions made by the system designer about each of these issues will determine how well the system works. To the extent that certain features are included or excluded, the general usefulness of the system and its appropriateness for specific applications will be determined. Many design decisions have implications for the type of hardware or software needed to run the system.

## USABILITY/USER INTERFACE: Beyond user friendly

Usability is an important dimension of any modern computer system. Software that is difficult to learn, frustrating or confusing to use, or results in an unduly large number of errors, is not acceptable. Hypertext systems, like all other software, must meet certain usability criteria.

Learning time must be minimal. By the use of menus (rather than command languages) and *default* options, it is possible for a novice to begin using a system immediately. The disk component of *Hypertext Hands-On!* illustrates this point—even a person with no computer background should be able to use it within a few minutes.

The design of the user interface should make errors unlikely. **Direct manipulation**{11} (the use of the mouse or touch) eliminates the possibility of errors from incorrectly typed commands. For example, you cannot get an error message using the *Hypertext Hands-On!* disk. Clear directions, help messages, and consistent system responses all reduce the likelihood of errors.

By following user interface design principles carefully, hypertext systems that are easy to use can be designed. These principles are based upon **human factors research**{144}. For more about user interface design, see Shneiderman (1987) in the **References**{137}.


## DISPLAYS: What you see is what you get

One of the major design (and implementation) issues in developing a hypertext system is the type of graphics display that will be used. The type of display chosen determines what kinds of **graphics**{67} and **screen formats**{64} are possible. It also determines what type of color and **windows**{9} will be possible as well as how much detail can be displayed (screen resolution).

In the domain of personal computers there are many different display standards currently in use, which presents a design dilemma. For example, IBM PCs and PS/2s support at least four types of color graphics (HGA, CGA, EGA, and VGA), which provide a range of screen resolution from $320 \times 200$ *pixels* to $640 \times 480$ pixels and colors that range from monochrome to 256 simultaneous shades. Displays can also vary considerably in size, ranging from the very small horizontal screens found on laptops to screens as large as 20 inches diagonally.

The displays used in engineering workstations, such as those made by Apollo and Sun, are usually large, high resolution screens with resolutions in the range of $1000 \times 1000$ pixels. This makes them ideally suited for hypertext delivery because a lot of information (especially graphics) can be displayed at one time. Unfortunately, such workstations are not widely found outside of research labs. On the other hand, the display capabilities of the popular IBM PC (in CGA mode) severely limit the type of graphics and color possible. Newer generations of personal computers such as the IBM PS/2 family and the Apple Macintosh II will help to expand the display capabilities of commercial hypertext systems.

For hypertext applications it is quite important to ensure good screen readability because users may spend many hours continuously reading text and looking at graphic images. Research results have demonstrated that many computer display screens can take 30% longer to read than printed text. If the studies include the additional time to turn pages, the confusion over page turning commands, and anxieties that some users have in reading from a computer, then task times can double. If you are considering using a hypertext system, you should push for the highest resolution displays possible.

However, there is good and growing evidence that higher resolution displays, techniques to improve fonts (such as antialiasing), and larger displays (more lines of text) can substantially reduce or eliminate the disadvantages associated with online reading. Designers and users are also encouraged to avoid use of text passages in upper case only, right justification with monospace fonts, flickering displays, and glare from ambient light.

There is controversy about the effects of many screen design variables, including certain colors of text and backgrounds, polarity (black on white vs. white on black), screen position (down and angled vs. eye-level and upright), single vs. double spacing, and line widths. These issues should be examined carefully when designing hypertext applications.

## PERFORMANCE: Faster is better

Performance of a hypertext system is measured in terms of response time. If the system is too slow, it becomes frustrating to use. Users generally prefer faster response time, even down to a tenth of a second. However, fast response times encourage the user to take less time to think, which can lead to errors or disorientation. Response times of less than a tenth of a second can cause confusion because screen changes may be difficult to perceive. Furthermore, novices sometimes prefer a slower pace so they can read at a leisurely pace.

Response time is a function of many factors of system and database design: the average **document size**{71}, total number of documents, **network**{41} facilities, type of **graphics**{67} involved, **search**{12} algorithms employed, type of storage used (i.e., magnetic versus optical disk), and amount of workstation storage.

Achieving satisfactory response time is critical to the **usability**{37} of a hypertext system. No matter how elegant or sophisticated the system is, if the response time is slow, the system will not be acceptable to users.

Increasing use of parallel and distributed processing architectures may be a significant factor in the performance of future hypertext systems. As **databases**{7} become larger (e.g., the contents of a full library), there will be millions of links to traverse across hundreds of computer systems. Parallel and distributed processing will make it possible to perform such searches quickly.

## PRINTING: Getting it on paper

Because hypertext involves the creation of nonlinear documents, translating hypertext into printed output (a linear process) is a significant challenge. When a hypertext document is printed, some convention for how to handle links is needed. In addition, formatting codes that specify type fonts and styles, line spacing, page width, and indentation are desirable.

One solution to the printing dilemma is simply to print documents in the order they are stored. For example, in a system such as **HyperCard**{89}, the standard printing capability is limited to images of the cards in the order they appear on the screen. In systems where the documents are organized **hierarchically**{6}, the printed listing may follow the hierarchy in terms of sequence of printing. Some systems allow the user to compose the output document by specifying database documents and their order. If the system allows **tours**{14} to be created, printing the tour provides a means of organizing the database for output.

Links may be shown in bold when printed (as they are in the book version of *Hypertext Hands-On!*). If the links are citations or notes, they may be printed as footnotes to the main text. In systems that feature multiple types of links, it may be possible to specify which links are to be printed.

For a discussion of what was involved in developing the print version of *Hypertext Hands-On!*, see the Epilog.

## VERSIONS: Preserving the pattern of changes

One major problem in hypertext systems is how to handle updates to the database. Should only one version of the database be kept, or should multiple versions be available? It may be important to be able to see previous versions of a document. In a system that allows **collaboration**{49}, it may be desirable to see the different versions created by each author.

There are two levels at which versions may be kept: the node/link level and the overall database. You may want to tag specific nodes with dates or author names as well as designating a date or name to the entire database. This raises the need to be able to access different versions and which versions are shown by default. It is also desirable to be able to **search**{12} for items according to version (e.g., All documents created after 1/6/88 or All documents created by Fred M.).

Another important aspect of updates to a hypertext database is letting the reader know that new versions exist. A capability is needed that lets users see all nodes and links that are new or have changed since their last access. This is similar to the facility provided on many forms of **electronic message**{73} systems that lets you read all new messages.

## NETWORKS: Communications across computers

Networks allow people to share access to hypertext databases. Network architectures have implications about how hypertext documents can be shared and what type of **collaboration**{49} is possible.

The oldest form of networking is time-sharing, in which terminals share a central processor and database. In more recent distributed networks, each work station or local processor contains its own database, and information is transferred between systems via packet-switched or local network techniques. Distributed networks make sharing of hypertext documents more complex because network addresses must be tracked and multiple copies of documents are likely to exist.

A major problem in networking is lack of **compatibility**{52} among different systems, making it difficult or impossible to share information. Hypertext systems such as **Xanadu**{78} and **Neptune**{86} attempt to overcome incompatibility problems by separating the machine-independent database from the machine-dependent user interface. This approach allows databases to be shared across multiple systems, while at the same time allowing them to be adapted to the input/output characteristics of each system.

## ANNOTATION: Users leave their marks

An important capability not present in most current hypertext systems is the ability of the user to make additions to documents. These additions might take the form of "margin notes" that are kept together with the document. Annotations may be shown along with the original document or in a **separate window**{9} when requested by the user.

Annotation capability is especially important in the **authoring**{60} process. A reviewer or editor needs to be able to make suggestions or corrections as part of the original text. To facilitate this, most manuscripts are double-spaced with wide margins. Until recently, this kind of "markup" capability has been missing from electronic documents.

One consideration in allowing any form of annotation capability is ensuring the integrity of the original documents. For example, if the application is **documentation**{29}, **instruction**{30}, a **medical text**{23}, or a **help system**{28}, it is important that the content not be modified so that it is incorrect or misleading. When hypertext is used as a communication medium or for **collaboration**{49}, annotation capability is extemely important so that participants can read each other's comments.

## INTEGRATION: Sharing the wealth

A major limitation of many hypertext systems is that they are completely self-contained. This means that all documents must be created and viewed within the context of that hypertext system. Obviously this is a problem in terms of widespread access and use of hypertext systems. For example, most computer users already have a variety of programs (such as text editors, database managers, spreadsheets) that they use to create and analyze information. To be useful, a hypertext system must be able to load information to and from these existing programs.

Some steps toward integrated environments have been taken in this direction by the **Intermedia**{79} and **HyperCard**{89} systems, but even these systems are limited in the degree of integration possible. Because each hypertext system developed to date has its own unique structure, there has been little opportunity to standardize on a hypertext format that could be read by other programs. This creates a significant **compatibility**{52} problem across different hypertext systems.

One interesting possibility that avoids the compatibility problem is the use of hypertext as a system manager that integrates all other programs running on a computer. The hypertext system can be used to provide a single consistent user interface for all other programs.

## ALIASING: Double the meaning, double the fun

A major problem in using a hypertext system is the failure to find desired information. A major cause of such search failures is that people use different terms than the assigned name of the item. Research has shown that search success rates can be increased from 20–80% if multiple names are allowed. This technique is called aliasing.

For best results, aliases should be determined empirically by discovering what alternate names users actually try to use. Aliasing capability can be built into a system so that it displays or asks for alternate terms when a search fails and automatically assigns to the original term the term selected or provided by the user.

Applying the aliasing technique to hypertext would imply that links should have alternate names provided by users. These names could be displayed when the user requests alternate names for a link as well as being used to match search requests.

For further discussion of aliasing, see Furnas, Landauer, Gomez, and Dumais (1987) in **References**{137}.

## FISHEYE VIEWS: Viewing in context

Historically, displays of information have provided an exact representation of the current document. If the display screen is relatively small and the database very large, **navigation**{49} through the database is difficult because only a small portion of the total database can be seen at once. The use of multiple **windows**{9} can help to some degree, but they also provide relatively small viewing areas.

The concept of the fisheye view is based upon the analogy of a fisheye camera lens, which distorts the image so that the nearest objects are seen in detail and distant objects are compressed. In the context of text documents, a fisheye view shows full details of the immediate location as well as outlines of other parts of the document. The fisheye view changes dynamically as the cursor location is changed.

Figure 3.1 shows a fisheye view of part of a C program. The program code at the current cursor location is shown in full (line number 39), whereas only the main procedure calls are shown for the rest of the program. This allows the programmer to "see" the entire program in relation to the current line. Applied to a hypertext database, the fisheye view would show all of the linked nodes working "outward" from the current node.

Although the fisheye approach cleverly solves some problems, it can be disconcerting. As the user moves the focus of attention the screen will change drastically, requiring a fresh effort at orientation. Furthermore, the user cannot make use of familiar patterns in the code because of

```
   1 #define DIG 40
   2 #include <stdio.h>
...4 main()
   5 {
   6        int c, i, x[DIG/4], t[DIG/4], k = DIG/4, noprint = 0;
...8        while((c=getchar()) != EOF){
   9            if(c >= '0' && c <= '9'){
..16            } else {
  17                switch(c){
  18                    case '+':
..27                    case '-':
..38                    case 'e':
>>39                        for(i=0;i<k;i++) t[i] = x[i];
  40                        break;
  41                    case 'q':
..43                    default:
..46                }
  47                if(!noprint){
..57                }
  58            }
  59            noprint = 0;
  60        }
  61 }
```

**Figure 3.1**   Fisheye view of a C program. (From *ACM SIGCHI 86 Proceedings*, Courtesy of ACM and the author.)

the selective display of noncontiguous lines. An alternate approach is a **hierarchical view**{45}. See Furnas (1986) in **References**{137}.

## HIERARCHICAL VIEWS: Seeing the forest for the trees

One of the great difficulties in **browsing**{10} any large body of information is gaining some overview and orientation. In a printed book, the size of the book gives some indication of the total volume of information. The book's table of contents conveys the structure of ideas imposed on the linear structure of the pages.

With electronic media, it is not automatically apparent how much information is available, how it is structured, and where the reader is currently. The fisheye view is one possible approach; hierarchical views are another possible solution. In a hierarchical view, the reader gets to see a high-level tree-structured index in one window, and by pointing at an item the user can view the contents of that document in another window. The user can scroll either window without affecting the contents of the other. The greater stability of the text and the simpler cognitive model may make the hierarchical view more attractive than the fisheye view in many applications. One variant of hierarchical browsing is to allow the user to open up levels in the index window, as is done in many of the outline or idea-processor programs.

Having both the high-level and detailed information on the screen at once has been demonstrated to be effective in program browsing. On the other hand, hierarchical views can be implemented only for hypertext databases that have a **hierarchical structure**{6}.

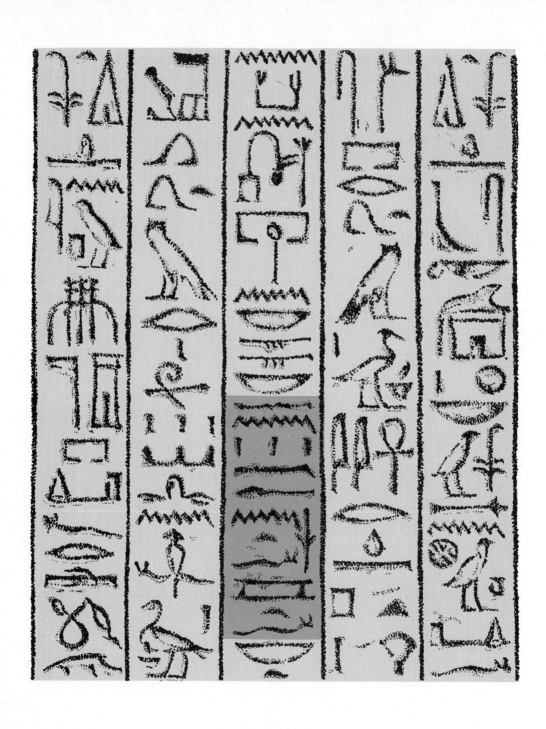

# Implementation
# Issues

**4**

## OVERVIEW

This chapter discusses issues in the implementation of hypertext systems, including **navigation**{49}, **collaboration**{49}, **security**{50}, **text
conversion**{51}, **compatibility**{52}, **rights**{53}, **public access**{54},
**publishing**{55}, and **usability evaluation**{56}. Implementation issues
arise when the system is put into regular use. The success or failure of
the system may depend upon how these issues are resolved.

The design of the system and the intended application(s) play a major
role in determining which implementation issues will be most critical
for a particular system. Hence the issues discussed in this chapter build
upon the information presented in Chapters 2 and 3.

## NAVIGATION: Lost in hyperspace

Getting lost in a hypertext database is a common and serious problem. There are two aspects to this problem: not being able to find desired information, and getting disoriented. Some hypertext systems use only single words for **link**{3} names, which does not provide much context for searching. Furthermore, if the database is poorly organized or organized for a different purpose than that of the current user, retrieval may be difficult.

Use of functional or alphabetical **indexing**{11} can make it easier to find information. The user should be able to return to a directory or home screen from any place in the document by selecting a "return" or "home" option. Some systems provide text string or keyword searching or "Goto" commands that allow the user to go directly to specified documents.

Disorientation occurs because users do not have enough information about their current location relative to the overall structure of the database. Most hypertext systems provide very little in the way of location cues. On the other hand, books provide page numbers and chapter headings as well as thickness that help readers determine where they are (or where they were).

There are a number of mechanisms that can be used to improve orientation in a hypertext system. Some systems provide a map or schematic of the database showing current location and past links selected (see **browsing**{10}). Allowing the user to place some form of **bookmarks**{14} makes it possible for the user to return to a specific location at any time. Use of color, icons, and **graphics**{67} helps to provide contextual clues that facilitate orientation. For more about navigation problems in hypertext, see Monty (1986) in **References**{137}.

## COLLABORATION: Working together

Hypertext pioneers envisioned that many people might work on the same document. Thus hypertext documents are dynamic not only because of links but also because the contents can be changed as they are read (see **annotation**{41}). Such a multiuser environment allows teams of authors to create a large database rapidly.

Collaboration raises many difficult technical issues. Is there only one **version**{40} of a document, or is there a version for each author? If there is only a single version, what happens if one author deletes portions that contain links to another author's documents? Does there need to be a way for authors to identify their contributions, or are all contributions treated anonymously?

One technique that has been used in some hypertext systems is to create a virtual copy of the document for each author based upon that author's changes. These virtual documents simply consist of change actions to the actual document, which are regenerated when the document is viewed. The benefit of this approach is that each author does not need a copy of the document, minimizing storage requirements. The difficultly is the time and computation involved in reconstituting a document.

Collaboration introduces issues having to do with legal **rights**{53} as well as **networks**{41}.

## SECURITY: Controlling access

In any publicly available hypertext system, security is a consideration. Typically, the originator of a document defines the type of access possible: read only, add but not change (see **annotation**{41}), change, copy, delete, or rename. All users may be granted the same level of access, or different individuals may be given different levels of access. Passwords may also be used to limit access to a system or to certain documents. Systems that feature security mechanisms usually have a *default* (e.g., read only) and may provide access control as an option for any document.

To some hypertext researchers, the idea of restricted access to documents is contrary to the philosophy of **collaboration**{49} and information sharing that underlies hypertext. However, most developers of public hypertext systems see security as a necessary measure to prevent misuse or abuse of a database.

## TEXT CONVERSION: From paper to electrons

The idea of linking up large hypertext databases to create global electronic libraries is one of the central ideas of hypertext visionaries such as **Bush**{99} and **Nelson**{100}. Thousands of large online **databases**{7} already exist and are available via information retrieval systems such as DIALOG, BRS, and Nexis/Lexis.

Putting these databases in hypertext format would be a monumental task. Links would need to be placed in each record (document) and **browsing**{10} capabilities added to these databases. If links were to be established across databases, they would need to have comparable structures.

It seems likely that many existing databases will be converted to hypertext form (see the discussion of the *OED*{21} and the AIRS **Bible**{32} projects). In some cases, only new records added to databases will contain coded links suitable for hypertext. Well structured documents with explicit organization are better prospects for conversion than are documents with unique structures. Hypertext systems such as **Xanadu**{78} have been designed to facilitate the creation of large-scale libraries; however, these systems do not deal with the text conversion problem very well.

In the domain of the personal computer, text conversion is much more feasible because most PC-based hypertext systems accept standard ASCII files as input. Existing electronic documents can be usually converted to ASCII format. This leaves the task of identifying links using the **authoring**{60} capabilities of the hypertext program.

Many documents to be converted contain various kinds of **graphics**{67}. The conversion of graphics to hypertext format is problematic. Formats of graphics files differ widely across systems. Modern *digitizing* or scanning technology makes it possible to convert most graphic images from paper to electronic form so they can be incorporated into hypertext databases. However, the degree of manipulation possible with the graphic once it is in electronic form (e.g., resizing, rotation, cropping, etc.) depends upon the **graphic editor**{69} available.

Digitizing technology can also be used to convert printed documents to electronic form. Optical character recognition (OCR) devices scan printed pages and create a text file. Although OCR devices do not produce 100% accurate conversions, they are a possible solution to the text-conversion problem.

## COMPATIBILITY: Every system is an island

Under the topic of system design, we discussed the issue of **integration**{42}, the ability of hypertext systems to work with other programs. A closely related implementation problem is the inability of hypertext programs to run on more than one type of computer system. As a rule, each system runs only on a specific type of hardware, under a specific operating system, with a unique **user interface**{37}. Consequently, moving the hypertext database from one system to another is difficult, if not impossible.

To the extent that hypertext databases are accessed via networks, the compatibility problem is reduced. However, each terminal or workstation must have the appropriate **display**{37} and **input**{65} capabilities. For example, a hypertext system that uses bit-mapped **graphics**{67} and assumes mouse input is not going to work on a nongraphics terminal that has only a keyboard for input.

There are two solutions to the compatibility dilemma. One solution is for hypertext system developers to implement their systems on multiple machines and terminals. Some systems, such as **Hyperties**{86} and **GUIDE**{88}, do run on more than one type of hardware. The other solution is to separate the underlying hypertext database from the user interface. **Xanadu**{78} and **Neptune**{86} are examples of systems that follow this approach.

# RIGHTS: Who owns what?

Like other new forms of electronic information, hypertext poses diffi-culties for copyright law. Copyright law is designed to protect the intellectual rights of an author on original works and all derivations. In the static world of print or photographic media, interpretation of unlawful reproduction is relatively straightforward. However, software and video media make this determination more difficult.

A problematic aspect of copyright for hypertext systems is multiau-thored documents. Some hypertext systems are designed to facilitate the **collaboration**{49} of many authors with no real attribution of authorship. Under these circumstances, establishing copyrights for participating authors is difficult. If royalty payments are involved for hypertext documents with multiple authors, it will be necessary to track the usage of each separately authored component.

In the case of hypermedia, establishment and enforcement of copy-right becomes even more complicated. If a passage of text is put in synthesized speech form is it still the same work? If a photograph or drawing is digitized and changed in significant ways (e.g., distorted or shaded) is it a derived work? If a set of still photographs is organized in a motion sequence, or if frames are dropped out of a motion sequence, are these new "performances" of the original work? There are no simple answers to these questions.

Beyond copyright issues, new issues of product liability are raised by hypertext. Is an author or publisher responsible for the validity of links if use of this information results in some form of catastrophe? For example, suppose a physician using a medical hypertext system makes a serious misdiagnosis due to an incorrect link between a symptom and a cause and is subsequently sued by the patient. Is the author or publisher of the hypertext system also liable for the mistake? This issue of product liability is a general one facing the software industry, but it is even more complex in the case of hypertext because of the enor-mous number of links possible and the difficulty of testing them all.

Finally, contracts and agreements involving hypertext systems may introduce new legal problems. One especially troublesome area for hypertext is contractual obligations regarding updates, enhancements, or new versions. Because most hypertext systems are in a constant state of change as new nodes or links are added, it is difficult to define distinct **versions**{40}, except by very arbitrary criteria (date, version numbers). On the other hand, a system could have major revisions that might not be easily discernable. Defining exactly what counts as an upgrade, new version, or major upgrade is difficult.

For further discussion of the legal issues associated with hypertext, see the article by Jones in the **Hypertext 87 Papers**{139}.

## PUBLIC ACCESS: Power to the people

If hypertext is to serve the same functions of information dissemination that are currently performed by print media such as books, newspapers, and **magazines**{111}, it will be necessary to make hypertext systems publicly accessible in libraries, schools, and offices. Even though an increasing number of individuals may own personal computers that allow them to use hypertext systems, others will need to have access provided in public places. For example, **Ted Nelson**{100} envisions neighborhood community centers where people would go to access or create databases.

Making hypertext publicly available puts emphasis on a high degree of **usability**{37}. It is not reasonable to require any form of training for a public hypertext system — it must be designed to work very simply and intuitively.

Making computer work stations available in sufficient quantities to meet public needs is likely to be a problem. Most libraries and schools have very limited budgets, and buying computers will be difficult to justify until hypertext systems provide clear-cut advantages. Availability of important publications in hypertext form (**encyclopedias**{22}, **dictionaries**{21}, or historical documents) would likely be a significant deciding factor.

Perhaps it will be necessary to treat hypertext systems as information utilities similar to electricity and telephone systems in order to ensure widespread public access. This would allow subsidization and standardization, which might facilitate widespread availability of the necessary technology.

## PUBLISHING: Dissemination of hypertext databases

Existing multiuser hypertext systems are privately accessed (restricted to a specific organization or group). Making hypertext systems public (unrestricted access) introduces many issues, such as **security**{50}, **collaboration**{49}, **compatibility**{52}, and **rights**{53}. Public hypertext systems must be distributed both geographically and organizationally. This means that such systems must be accessible across a broad range of computers and terminals (the compatibility problem).

To be most useful, published hypertext documents need to allow links within the document itself, not just to the document itself. This allows readers to disagree with specific items through **annotations**{41} that can be viewed by all subsequent readers. All references should also link to their sources so that a reader can examine the original sources directly.

The ideal scenario for hypertext publishing is the capability to go into a library (or use a home computer), sign on to a system, and begin to browse in a completely unrestricted fashion. The system automatically takes care of shifting from computer to computer where specific hypertext databases are stored.

In order to deal with the immensity of such global databases, **filters**{13} will become essential. Readers must be able to specify the topics they are, and are not, interested in.

# USABILITY EVALUATION: Measuring ease of use

Usability has already been mentioned as a critical attribute of hypertext systems. Informal opinions about the "user friendliness" of a **user interface**{37} are being replaced by more formal approaches to measurement. Objective criteria for user interfaces are carefully applied to specific user populations and specific tasks. These criteria include

1. time to learn

2. speed of performance on benchmark tasks

3. rate and distribution of errors

4. human retention over time

Subjective criteria can be assessed by semantic differential scales such as: Did you find the error messages to be (1) clear. . . (5) confusing? Topics for subjective evaluation might include readability of the screen; appropriateness of colors; meaningfulness of abbreviations or terminology; clarity of screen layout or screen sequences; utility of instructions, online help text, and error messages; pace of the interaction; and efficacy of the user guides. Kent Norman, John Chin, and Ben Shneiderman at the University of Maryland have developed a standardized Questionnaire for User Interface Satisfaction (QUIS), which assesses variables such as these. Subjective satisfaction should be high for hypertext systems because usage is often discretionary and therefore dissatisfied users will avoid using them.

Corporations and government agencies are increasingly relying on usability laboratories to conduct empirical evaluations of software user interfaces. Often equipped with videotaping facilities, these labs give researchers and developers a chance to study people attempting to use hypertext systems under realistic conditions. To date, hypertext usability studies have usually been a blend of informal performance evaluation and subjective commentary. Leading research centers are beginning to conduct rigorous studies.

See **Human Factors Research**{144} for more information about usability evaluation.

# 5

# Authoring

## OVERVIEW

The process of creating hypertext documents and databases is called authoring. This chapter discusses major aspects of authoring, including **structuring hyperknowledge**{61}, **authoring principles**{62}, **authoring tools**{63}, **screen formats**{64}, **input modes**{65}, **graphics** {67}, **sound/speech**{68}, **text editors**{68}, **graphic editors**{69}, the **root document**{71}, **document size**{71}, **cognitive processes**{72}, and **electronic messaging**{73}.

The hypertext author must make a series of decisions about how to organize the entire database and individual documents. The design of the system (Chapter 3) determines what features will be available to the author. Implementation decisions (Chapter 4) also influence the authoring process.

For a discussion about the authoring of *Hypertext Hands-On!*, see the Epilog.

# STRUCTURING HYPERKNOWLEDGE: Exploiting the medium

Throughout history, authors have learned ways to structure knowledge to suit the linear print medium. When appropriate, authors have explored strategies for linking related fragments of text and graphics even in the linear format. Now, hypertext encourages the nonlinear interconnection of links among nodes.

Restructuring knowledge to suit this new medium is a fascinating experience. The first challenge is to structure the knowledge in a way that an overview can be presented to the reader in the **root document**{71} or introductory article. The overview should identify the key subsidiary ideas and the breadth of coverage. Books present a clear vision of their boundaries and readers can know when they have read it all, but in the hypertext world other mechanisms must be created to give the reader a sense of progress and closure.

The overall structure of a document set must make sense to readers so that they can form a mental model of the topics covered. This facilitates traversal of the database and reduces disorientation.

When writing articles, the hypertext author is freer to use high-level concepts and terminology. Novices can select the terms to learn about, whereas knowledgeable readers can move ahead to more complex topics. For example, in a historical database, key events, people, or places can be mentioned without description, and novices can follow the links to read the articles in related nodes if they need background material.

Finally, hypertext is conducive to the inclusion of appendices, examples, background information, original sources, bibliographic references, and so on. Interested readers can pursue the details; casual readers can ignore them.

# AUTHORING PRINCIPLES: The art and the craft

Creating documents for a hypertext database introduces some additional considerations beyond the usual concerns of good writing (such as use of simple sentences, active voice, and no jargon). These additional considerations include:

1. *Chunking* — The information to be presented needs to be organized into small "chunks" that deal with one topic, theme, or idea. Each chunk represents a node or document in the database.

2. *Interrelationships* — Each document should contain links to other documents. The more links contained in the documents, the richer the connectivity of the hypertext database. On the other hand, avoid gratuitous links — each link should serve a clear purpose.

3. *Consistency of document names* — It is important to keep a list of names given to documents as they are created; otherwise, it becomes difficult to identify links properly. Synonyms are to be encouraged (as long as they are kept track of).

4. *Master reference list* — Create a master reference list as you author to ensure correct citations and prevent redundant or missing citations.

5. *Simplicity in traversal* — **Navigation**{49} should be simple, intuitive, and consistent throughout the system. Movement through the system should be effortless and should not require thought.

6. *Screen design* — Screens should be designed so they can be grasped perceptually. Visual layout is very important in screen design.

7. *Low cognitive load* — Minimize the burden on the user's short-term memory. Do not require the user to remember things from one screen to another.

8. *Early reviews* — Subject the database to technical, legal, and management reviews as early as possible. As the database becomes larger, changes become more difficult to make.

9. *Maintain multiple perspectives* — When authoring, try to balance the technical requirements of the system with the user's perspective and the organizational use of the database.

## AUTHORING TOOLS: Hypertext construction sets

Each hypertext system includes a set of authoring tools, which are used to create the documents, links, and index entries. Some important considerations are:

1. ease in specifying links

2. capability to switch between author mode and user mode to test ideas

3. explicit or automatic saving

4. range of editing functions available (i.e., copying, moving, insertion, deletion, etc.)

5. availability of lists of link names and index terms

6. range of screen formatting commands available

7. capability to import existing text or graphic files

8. availability of search/replace functions for making changes

9. control of color (text, background)

10. capability to export files to other systems

11. capability to run other programs (e.g., spreadsheet or animation)

12. support for **CD-ROM**{15} and videodisc.

Each hypertext system includes its own authoring tools. The authoring capabilities of Hyperties are described in the appendix.

One of the more interesting hypertext authoring tools currently available is HyperTalk, the authoring language that underlies **Hyper-Card**{89}. HyperTalk allows you to write scripts that send messages between HyperCard objects (buttons, fields, backgrounds, cards, and stacks). You can define links, accept input, display information, perform calculations, and specify conditional actions (i.e., "If this, THEN do that"). Here is an example of a HyperTalk script that defines the dial button on the Phone card:

```
on MouseUp
   if first char of the message box is in "0123456789("
   then dial the message box
   else
     Ask "Dial what number?"
     dial it
   end if
end MouseUp
```

Availability of an authoring tool such as HyperTalk allows for more complex links and interactions in a hypertext system.

To the extent that the authoring tools determine what can be created in a hypertext database and how effectively, the capabilities available are very important. On the other hand, adherence to appropriate authoring principles is also critical to the effectiveness of hypertext databases and is independent of the authoring tools used.

## SCREEN FORMATS: Designing the layout

In designing hypertext screens, a number of formatting and organizational issues arise. Some of these issues are a function of authoring principles; others are determined by computer capabilities.

Spacing of lines and the amount of information to be included on a single display are a major concern because of the poor readability of many computer screens (up to 30% slower to read than printed text). A major principle of screen design is that displays should not be "cluttered" and contain too much information. Resolution and size of the screen **display**{37} affect how much information can be shown at once; higher resolution and larger screens allow more information.

The use of scrolling and **windows**{9} also affects information organization. With scrolling, documents are continuous and can be viewed a line at a time under the control of the user. In some systems, the viewing windows can be resized and relocated by the user. With control of scrolling and windows, users can adjust the information presented to suit their own tastes.

When the user can create multiple windows on the screen at the same time, the issue arises as to what should be displayed in different windows. For example, should the user be allowed to see the same document in multiple windows in order to compare different portions? Should the user be able to specify that when a link is activated, it appears in an adjacent window instead of replacing the current document? Should it be possible to designate one window for **browsing**{10} only? These are examples of the many questions that windowing capability raises for the hypertext author or system designer.

For more about screen formatting, see Brown (1988) in **References**{137}.

## INPUT MODES: Mousing around

There are four ways to input information into a computer system: typing, **direct manipulation**{11}, scanning, and voice recognition. Each has its advantages and disadvantages.

Until recently, typing on a keyboard has been the usual way of entering commands or responses. The keyboard is a relatively standardized input device that has been in use for many decades (on typewriters). For fast typists, it allows rapid input of information (50–150 words per minute). However, typed input also leads to the use of complex command languages that require substantial learning and are error-prone.

With the popularity of the mouse, direct manipulation input has become commonplace. Touch screens have been available for many years, but they have not become as popular as the mouse, although in some instances they result in faster or easier input. Improved touch screen strategies and technology may lead to more widespread use. The major advantage of pointing input is that it eliminates the need to learn and remember a command language—all responses can be selected from choices presented on the screen. The limitation of pointing input is that it does not accommodate data entry tasks very well.

In the context of hypertext, input via pointing seems to be the easiest way for a user to select links and commands. For this reason, most hypertext systems are designed to work with direct manipulation input. On the other hand, authoring relies heavily on keyboard input, although the use of pointing for commands and operations can speed up the process.

Scanning refers to the digitization of text or graphics. There are many types of relatively inexpensive scanners available for personal computers that can translate a page of printed text or an illustration into a computer file. For the **conversion of text materials**{51} that already exist in printed form, scanning can save considerable time.

Voice input has been under development for many years. Although it is possible for a computer to recognize reliably a small number of words or phrases (100–200) from a specific individual, the general capability to recognize conversational discourse from any speaker is still a research area.

It is interesting to ponder how the availability of voice input might change hypertext systems. For example, a link could be activated by saying "Show me more about touch input" or "Take me back to the article about hypermedia." Such a system would need extremely good capability of understanding natural language—considerably beyond what is practical with current **artificial intelligence**{119} techniques. However, even existing discrete word recognition systems could handle the limited command and link terms found on a Hyperties screen: "next," "back," "speech," and so on.

# GRAPHICS: A picture is worth 1K words

New computer **displays**{37} are opening up exciting possibilities for graphics (i.e., the capability to show diagrams, schematics, photographs, etc.). With the advent of higher resolution screens (i.e., displays larger than 640 × 480 pixels) and more powerful microprocessors, it has become possible to improve vastly the display capabilities of computers.

Because of the historical limitations on displaying graphics, most early hypertext systems focused on text only. However, current systems such as **NoteCards**{82}, **HyperCard**{89}, and **Intermedia**{79} provide good graphics display capabilities as well as **graphics editors**{69} that facilitate the creation of graphics.

Although almost all current hypertext systems allow a link to point to a graphic as well as text (the *Hypertext Hands-On!* disk provides a number of examples), the more interesting capability is links that are in graphic form themselves. For example, pointing to a specific part of a diagram or schematic results in an enlargement of that area.

Another form of graphic displays that has come to be popular is *icons*. Icons are visual symbols for entities (e.g., files, programs) or actions (e.g., delete, copy, quit). To date, icons have not been widely used in hypertext systems to represent data, but this is possible. For example, imagine a weather map with icons for wind speed, precipitation, storm fronts, and so on. Or how about a directory or catalog where icons are used for each major kind of service or product?

Animation is becoming increasingly common but has not yet appeared in many hypertext systems (an exception is **HyperCard**{89}). Animation is the capability to show motion sequences. There are many hypertext applications where it would be desirable to show dynamic events (e.g., equipment operation, biological processes, repair procedures, etc.). Although this can sometimes be accomplished via video sequences stored on **CD-ROM**{15}, animation provides additional capabilities. Ideally, a hypertext animation sequence could be stopped and linked to another sequence or node in the database.

## SOUND/SPEECH: The end of the silent screen

Hypermedia allows sound or speech to be incorporated in a document. This could take the form of music, sound effects, or narration. (Instead of icons, we could have "earcons.") Sound/speech can be recorded and stored in digital form on **CD-ROM**{15}. Speech can also be synthesized from text.

Starting a sound/speech sequence is relatively straightforward, but it is unclear how to embed links within the sound/speech sequence itself. One possible technique is to show a symbol on the screen when the current portion of the sound/narrative has a link to another node. Other standard hypertext operations such as searching, indexing, and browsing are also problematic in the context of sound/speech sequences.

Authoring sound/speech is difficult because all references are likely to be codes that define the beginning and end of time sequences. The use of musical and phonetic notation for generated sound/speech sequences overcomes this problem and makes a good argument for the use of synthesized music and speech in hypertext databases. Although sound/speech enriches the user's experience, it adds complexity to the authoring process.

## TEXT EDITORS: Word games

A text editing program allows you to create and modify a document. Text editing programs are commonly called word processing programs (although technically speaking, a text editor does not also include the formatting capabilities of a word processing program). The basic functions of a traditional text editor are insert, delete, move, copy, find, and replace. These functions can apply at the character, paragraph, and page levels. Spelling checkers and thesauri are also included with some text editors.

When documents are printed, the text editor automatically controls the pagination of the document. The page length, line width, justification, hyphenation, line spacing, page numbering, and use of headers/footers can be specified. In more recent text editors that incorporate desktop publishing capabilities, typographic control is available, including the style and size of the type and even character spacing ("kerning").

Traditional text editors are controlled by commands embedded in the document. For example, to set the page length to 66 lines, a command such as ".pl 66" might be inserted at the beginning of the document. Similar commands are inserted for centered text, underlining, tabs, and so on. Newer text editors that are designed for *high resolution graphic* **displays**{37} feature WYSIWYG (What You See Is What You Get) capability (i.e., you see all changes on the screen as they are made).

Documents for many hypertext systems are prepared using a text editor. The resulting text files are loaded into a hypertext database using hypertext **authoring tools**{63} where special codes are inserted to indicate links and structural organization of the database. Some hypertext systems include their own built-in text editor, although these editors are not usually as powerful as separate text editing programs. For example, in the development of *Hypertext Hands-On!*, we used a powerful word processing program (XyWrite) to prepare the printed form (see the discussion in the Epilog). Some designers of text editors are beginning to add hypertext features.

## GRAPHICS EDITORS: Making pictures

Graphics editors make it easy for you to draw diagrams, illustrations, schematics, and sketches. The usual functions include copy, move, duplicate, rotate, erase, paint (fill), and scale (resize), as well as tools to draw lines, boxes, circles, or irregular shapes (freehand drawing). Figure 5.1 shows the main display of the graphics editor (Dr. Halo) used to create some of the graphics included on the *Hypertext Hands-On!* disk.

There are two different types of images that you can create: bit-mapped images and object-oriented images. In a bit-mapped image, every bit is included in the graphic and the entire graphic is considered a single entity. In an objected-oriented image, each component is an entity that can be manipulated; the graphic is a collection of objects instead of a single entity. Most editors create either bit-mapped or object-oriented graphics but not both.

"Cut and paste" is also an important capability of a graphics editor. Analogous to its function in a text editor, it allows the capability to define a region in a bit-mapped image or a set of objects and place it in a temporary storage area (often called a clipboard or scratchpad). The contents of the temporary storage can then be "pasted" into a different graphic.

Most recent graphics editors will accept a digitized image from a scanner (provided it has the correct file format). This means that a graphics editor can be used to modify photographic images as well as line drawings.

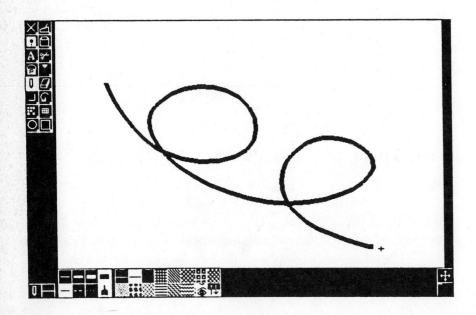

**Figure 5.1**   Graphics editor screen (Dr. Halo).

## ROOT DOCUMENT: It all starts here

The root document is very important because it helps you access other parts of the hypertext database easily. The root document is the first document you see when you start up a hypertext database. In **Hyperties**{86}, the root document is called the Introductory article; in **HyperCard**{89}, it is called the Home card.

There are several authoring strategies for creating the root document.

1. Make the root document an overview that contains **links**{3} to all major concepts in the database (glossary approach).

2. Adopt a **hierarchical**{45} approach in which the links in the root document are major categories (top-down approach).

3. Organize the root document as a list or table of contents of the major concepts in the database (menu approach).

4. Make the root document into a **tour**{14} of the database (tutorial approach).

The suitability of these different authoring strategies will depend upon the purposes and anticipated use of the database. In *Hypertext Hands-On!*, we have used the last approach (a tour) for the root document (the Introduction).

## DOCUMENT SIZE: Small is beautiful

A major concern when authoring hypertext documents is the optimal length of documents. Research results suggest that many short documents are preferable to a smaller number of long documents.

An experiment was performed by students at the University of Maryland using the **Hyperties**{86} system in which the same database was created as 46 short articles from 4 to 83 lines long and as 5 articles of 104 to 150 lines. Participants in the study were asked to answer multiple choice questions using the database during a time limited to 30 minutes. The 16 participants working with the short articles answered more questions correctly and took less time to answer the questions.

The effects of article length are influenced by screen size, nature of task, session duration, and experience of user. One consequence of many small articles is that it may increase **navigation**{49} problems.

## COGNITIVE PROCESSES: Links in the mind

From the earliest literature on hypertext (e.g., the article "As we may think" by **Vannevar Bush**{99}), writers have emphasized that hypertext matches human cognition, in particular, the organization of memory as a semantic network in which concepts are linked together by associations. Of course, hypertext databases do not really resemble human memory precisely because they lack the rich set of semantic associations (i.e., meaningful connections) that come from life experiences.

From the perspective of learning theory, hypertext should improve learning because it focuses attention on the relationships between ideas rather than on isolated facts. The associations provided by links in a hypertext database should facilitate remembering, concept formation, and understanding.

In addition, the greater sense of control over the reading process may produce increased involvement and desire to read more. In the same way that computer games can be very absorbing because of the high level of interactivity, hypertext databases may be very engaging too. For example, in a study at the University of Maryland supervised by the senior author, 8 of 20 participants preferred a hypertext version of a database, while only 4 preferred the paper version.

The authoring challenge is to design the structure of the hypertext database to match the ways that a user might want to think about the topics. To do this successfully, considerable experience in teaching or explaining the subject matter is needed to know the many ways that concepts might be related. Knowledge must be structured in a way that supports the mental models that readers may create when they use the hypertext system.

# ELECTRONIC MESSAGING: Telecommunicating

Many hypertext databases are the result of **collaboration**{49} among a group of authors at different locations. Such group authoring efforts are aided considerably by the use of electronic mail and conferencing over a **network**{41}. For this reason, electronic messaging is often an important aspect of the hypertext authoring process.

Electronic mail involves the exchange of messages between two or more individuals. Messages are sent instantaneously and can be read as soon as they are "posted" by the sender. These messages can be stored and kept as online correspondence files.

Electronic conferencing also involves the exchange of messages between two or more individuals. However, unlike mail, the messages are not private and can be viewed by anyone involved in the conference. In addition, conferences may be "real-time," in which all participants are signed on at the same time and messages are read as soon as they are posted.

Electronic messaging allows authors to have a high level of interaction without the need to be in the same location or to coordinate schedules. Lessons learned about the design and use of electronic message systems in past studies of computer conferencing may be valuable to hypertext system authors and designers.

A discussion of the role of electronic mail in the authoring of *Hypertext Hands-On!* is provided in the Epilog. See Kerr and Hiltz (1982) in **References**{137} for more information about collaboration via electronic message systems.

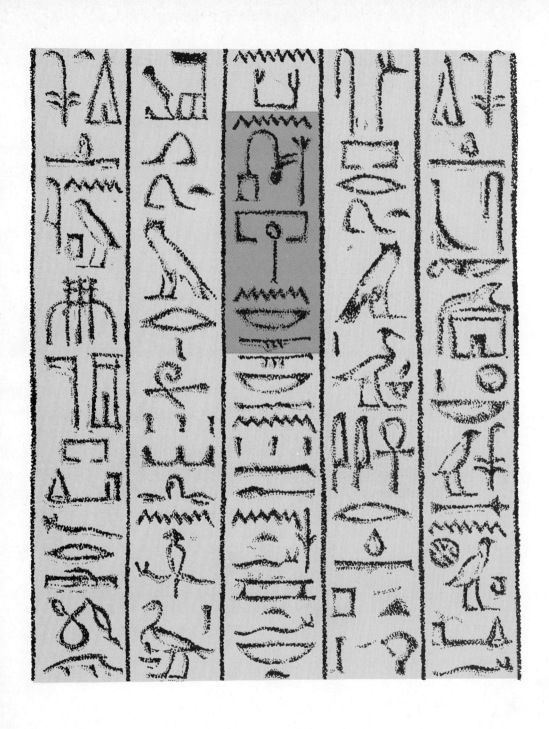

# Systems

**6**

## OVERVIEW

This chapter describes hypertext systems, including pioneering efforts such as **MEMEX**{77}, **XANADU**{78}, **AUGMENT**{78} (originally called NLS), and **KMS**{83} as well as more recent programs for personal computers, including **HyperCard**{89}, **NaviText**{91}, **Black Magic** {92}, **askSam**{92}, and **KnowledgePro**{94}. Some systems described (such as **Intermedia**{79}, **NoteCards**{82}, **Neptune**{86}, **WE**{88}) are primarily designed for research. Other systems, such as **GUIDE**{72} and **Hyperties**{86}, began as research systems but have also become commercial products. We have provided the company addresses for all systems that run on IBM PCs to make it easy for readers who want to **pursue hypertext further**{125}.

The systems mentioned in this section represent only a sample of the hypertext programs that have been developed. Others are described in the **Hypertext 87 Papers**{139} and Conklin (1987) in the **References**{137}.

# MEMEX: Bush's seminal vision

In 1945 an article titled "As we may think" was published in the magazine *Atlantic Monthly*. The article, written by **Vannevar Bush**{99}, a science advisor to President Roosevelt, proposed a major effort to automate technical literature. He described a machine called "memex" that would let an individual browse and create a multimedia library of technical documents including personal notes, photographs, and sketches. Bush was writing before computers as we know them had been invented. His plan for the machine involved the use of microfilm and photocell technologies.

Here is how Bush described the use of memex:

> The owner of the memex, let us say, is interested in the origin and properties of the bow and arrow. Specifically he is studying why the short Turkish bow was apparently superior to the English long bow in the skirmishes of the Crusades. He has dozens of possibly pertinent books and articles in his memex. First he runs through an encyclopedia, finds an interesting but sketchy article, leaves it projected. Next, in a history, he finds another pertinent item, and ties the two together. Thus he goes, building a trail of many items. Occasionally, he inserts a comment of his own, either linking it into the main trail or joining it by a side trail to a particular item. When it becomes evident that the elastic properties of available materials had a great deal to do with the bow, he branches off on a side trail which takes him through textbooks on elasticity and tables of physical constants. He inserts a page of longhand analysis of his own. Thus he builds a trail of his interest through the maze of materials available to him. [Bush, 1945, p. 107]

Memex encompassed the most important element of hypertext: **links**{3} between documents. In memex, the reader viewed two documents on separate screens and then typed in the name of the link in a code space. Once the link was established, activating a button on the machine while viewing one document would produce the other document. The implementation of this idea had to wait almost two decades!

For further discussion of memex, see Bush (1945) in **References**{137}.

## XANADU: Nelson's grand plan

**Ted Nelson**{100} introduced the term "hypertext" in his spirited, non-linear books in the 1960s. He has been developing the XANADU system for many years based upon his vision of hypertext. XANADU is a "global literary system" spanning a vast "docuverse" enabling widespread access to and sharing of the world's literature. Nelson explains the significance of hypertext as a mechanism for reducing the information explosion because in a hypertext system only the original document and changes to it are stored (instead of many redundant copies).

The XANADU system has been implemented in UNIX and is available in several forms. The system is intended to provide a machine-independent database server that can be connected up to a specific machine and **user interface**{37}. The specifications for the XANADU database protocol have been made public to encourage adoption. Nelson envisions the proliferation of online libraries all able to exchange information by means of the XANADU system. In 1988, AutoDesk, Inc., the developers of the highly successful AutoCad system, invested in the XANADU Operating Company, providing it with additional financial and technical support. For more information about Xanadu, see Nelson (1981) in **References**{137}.

## AUGMENT: Engelbart makes it work

AUGMENT is a **text editing**{68} system marketed by McDonnell Douglas for a multiuser **network**{41} environment. The system was originally called NLS and was developed at SRI International in the 1960s under the direction of **Douglas Engelbart**{101}. AUGMENT evolved from an experimental system intended to facilitate the activities of "knowledge workers" (people whose primary role is to process information) and tasks such as planning, analysis, and problem solving. Electronic messaging via *packet switched* networks is another essential component of the AUGMENT system.

AUGMENT uses a powerful command language for file-addressing operations. Links are identified by parenthesized file addresses, and a reader can jump to these new files by selecting the addresses. Linked files can also have links, and it is possible to skip from link to link using jump commands. Paths consisting of a series of file names can be specified as well.

AUGMENT features user-controlled **windows**{9}. A user can specify how many lines or what level of the file should be displayed. The reader can also specify a **filter**{13} that causes the system to display only files with the specified content.

One of the strengths of the AUGMENT system is the many features it provides for **collaboration**{49}. The capabilities include **electronic messages**{73}, archived messages (called the Journal), and shared-screen teleconferencing. All shared messages have the properties of standard files and can be linked.

Even though AUGMENT does not feature the bit-mapped **displays**{37} available in more modern hypertext systems, it does illustrate how a sophisticated command language can provide full hypertext capabilities. Engelbart's demonstration of the AUGMENT system at the 1968 Spring Joint Computer Conference was a major milestone in the history of hypertext. For further discussion of Augment, see Engelbart (1984) in **References**{137}.

## INTERMEDIA: Hypermedia demonstrated

One of the oldest hypertext research groups is the interdisciplinary Institute for Research and Scholarship (IRIS) at Brown University. A number of innovative hypertext systems have been developed at Brown under the leadership of **Andries van Dam**{102} including the original Hypertext Editing System (1968), the File Retrieval and Editing System (FRESS) from 1969 to 1982, and the Electronic Document System (1982).

INTERMEDIA is the current system under development. It is a hypermedia system designed for multimedia documents. Unlike past systems, INTERMEDIA is intended to be an environment that allows different types of applications (e.g., word processors, database programs, various editors, etc.) to be linked together rather than a closed system that allows links within only a single program. Some of the applications available include a **text editor**{68}, a **graphics editor**{69}, a timeline editor, a scanned image viewer, and a 3D image viewer. Figure 6.1 illustrates an INTERMEDIA screen with different applications in each **window**{9}.

A major concept in the organization of INTERMEDIA documents is the *web*. Every link belongs to one or more webs and can only be seen when the web that it belongs to is active. To view documents, the user must select a particular web. Webs provide a way of making links context dependent.

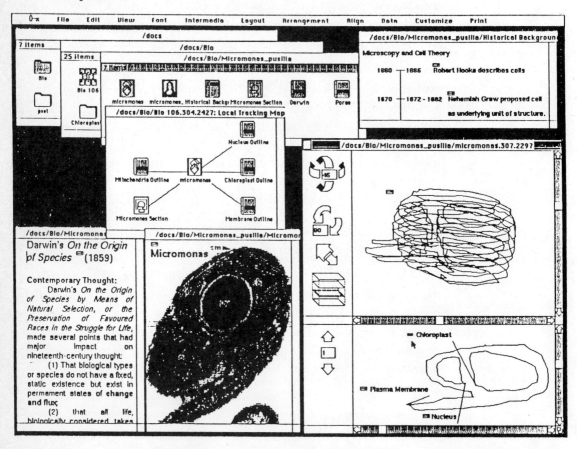

**Figure 6.1** Intermedia screen showing different application programs. (Reprinted from *IEEE Computer*, September 1987. Copyright 1987, IEEE.)

INTERMEDIA is intended as a tool for professors to organize and present material and for students to study and create reports. It has been used in two courses, English literature and biology (see **Instruction**{30}). See Yankelovich, Meyrowitz, and van Dam (1985) in **References**{137} for more information about INTERMEDIA.

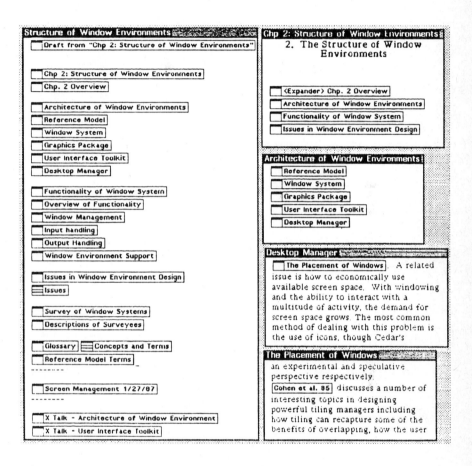

**Figure 6.2**  NoteCards screen showing notecards, fileboxes, and links. (From *Hypertext 87 Proceedings*.)

## NOTECARDS: Xerox creates an original

NoteCards is an experimental hypertext system developed at Xerox Palo Alto Research Center that runs on Xerox workstations. The system was primarily developed to support information-analysis tasks, including reading, categorization, interpretation, and technical writing.

A NoteCards database consists of four basic elements: notecards, **links**{3}, **browsers**{10}, and fileboxes. Figure 6.2 shows notecards (bottom right windows), links (boxed text) and fileboxes (left window and top two right windows) from a NoteCard screen. Figure 6.3 illustrates the NoteCards browser.

NoteCards are intended to be an electronic analog of a 3 × 5 card. Each notecard has a title and an arbitrary amount of space. Cards can be defined as different types (e.g., text, sketch, graph, etc.). When a card is opened, the appropriate type of editor is automatically loaded.

NoteCards runs under *LISP* and provides a programmer's interface and LISP functions to extend or customize NoteCard functions. For example, a program could be written for a bibliographic database that would create a filebox for each new reference, use the title of the reference as the filebox name, and create a link between the filebox and all other cards that cite that reference.

NoteCards is very rich in features and runs on a powerful workstation. However, the high price of the system and its complexity limit the potential for widespread distribution of NoteCards outside of the research community. For more about NoteCards, see Halasz, Moran, and Trigg (1987) and Halasz (1988) in **References**{137}.

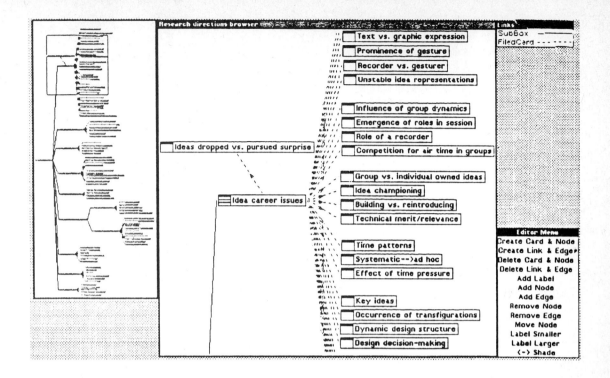

**Figure 6.3**   NoteCards screen showing browser. (From *Hypertext 87 Proceedings*.)

## KMS: The Knowledge Management System

KMS is a commercial hypermedia system marketed by Knowledge Systems, Inc. that runs on Sun and Apollo workstations. KMS is based upon the ZOG system developed at Carnegie Mellon University from 1976 to 1984. KMS/ZOG systems have been applied to a wide range of applications including project management, technical manuals, policy guidelines, and electronic publishing.

The basic element of a KMS database is called a "frame," which can contain text, graphics, or digitized images. Each frame has a name, title, body, tree items, annotation items, and command line (see Figure 6.4). The tree items serve as **links**{3} to other frames as shown in Figure 6.5. The annotation items can be used to provide comments, formatting instructions, or cross-reference links.

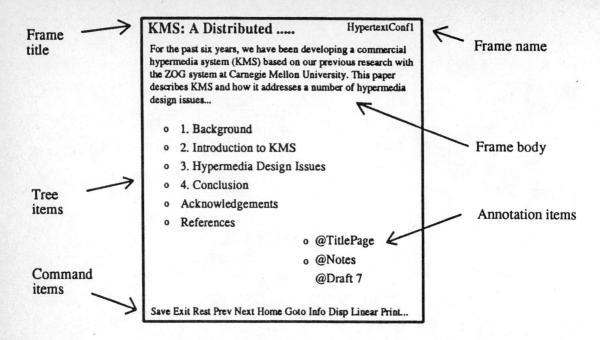

**Figure 6.4**    Sample KMS frame. (From *Hypertext 87 Proceedings*.)

The **user interface**{37} of KMS has some interesting design features. User control is almost completely via **direct manipulation**{11} using a three-button mouse. The functions of the mouse buttons are dynamic (i.e., constantly changing), and this allows the mouse to have broad functionality. KMS makes no distinction between navigating and editing; users can make changes to a frame at any time, and these changes are saved automatically. KMS does not support **windows**{9}; however, two frames can be displayed side by side.

Another important feature of KMS is that it is designed for **collaboration**{49} in a multiuser network. Because there is no separation between readers and authors in KMS, any and all changes made by one user are seen by all other users. One problem this introduces in the multiuser setting is interference between two people trying to make changes to the same frame at the same time. Many systems "lock out" all other users when one user is making changes to a document; KMS relies on the low probability of such incidents and informal notes posted by users that they are currently editing a frame.

See the articles about KMS by McCracken, Akscyn, and Yoder in **Hypertext 87 Papers**{139} and by McCracken and Akscyn (1984) and Akscyn, McCracken and Yoder (1988) in **References**{137}.

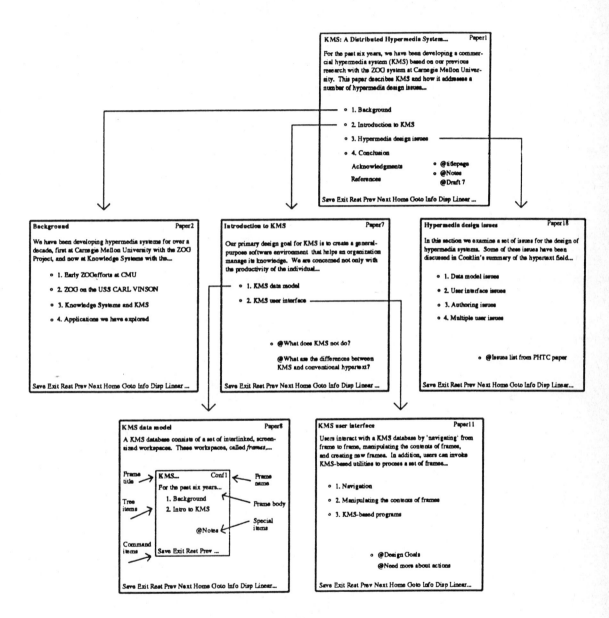

**Figure 6.5** Example of links in KMS. (From *Hypertext 87 Proceedings*.)

## HYPERTIES: The interactive encyclopedia

HYPERTIES (originally called TIES — The Interactive Encyclopedia System) has been under development at the University of Maryland since 1983 under the direction of **Ben Shneiderman**{104}. Early versions of the system were implemented in APL and C by Dan Ostroff.

The system has been used in a wide range of applications including **museum exhibits**{33} on the Holocaust, archeology, and photography; an online maintenance manual; orientations to the university student union and computer science department; and an introduction to database searching for a major library.

Many research studies have been conducted using the system. Some of the factors investigated include: **input modes**{65} (arrow keys versus mouse versus touch), explicit versus embedded menus, text density, **window**{9} size, and **indexing**{11} methods.

The commercial version of Hyperties has been implemented for the IBM PC; a research version runs on SUN 3 and 4 workstations. The IBM PC version of the Hyperties browser is used for the *Hypertext Hands-On!* disk (see **About Hyperties on the PC**{132}). The SUN 3 version uses the NEWS environment and has much more powerful windowing capabilities.

See Shneiderman (1987) in **References**{137} for further discussion about the development of Hyperties. For more information about Hyperties on the PC, contact Cognetics Corporation, 55 Princeton-Hightstown Rd., Princeton Jct., NJ 08550. (609) 799-5005.


## NEPTUNE: Software engineering tool

Neptune is a hypertext system developed by Tektronix to explore the application of hypertext to **software engineering**{31}. A database called DynamicDesign has been implemented using Neptune for the C programming environment.

The design of Neptune separates the **user interface**{37} (implemented in the *Smalltalk* language) from the hypertext processor called Hypertext Abstract Machine (HAM). This separation allows the nature of the user interface and the structure of the hypertext database to be modified independently. HAM consists of a broad range of hypertext constructs that permit it to model other hypertext databases.

HAM allows multiple **versions**{40} of nodes and links to be defined and keeps track of the version of any node or link. Versioning capability is especially important for software engineering databases because of the high frequency of change involved. In addition, the **browsing**{10} capability of the Neptune system is especially powerful (see Figure 6.6). See the article by Campbell and Goodman in **Hypertext 87 Papers**{139} for more information about Neptune and HAM.

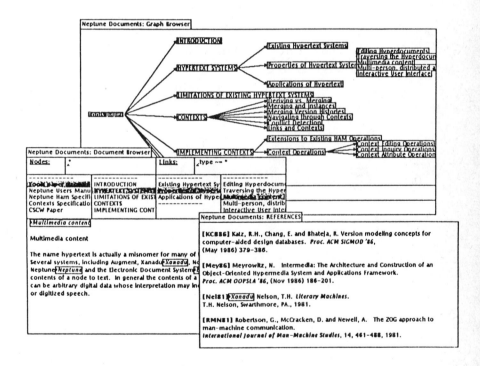

**Figure 6.6** Browsers in Neptune system. (Reprinted from *IEEE Computer*, September 1987. Copyright 1987, IEEE.)

## WE: Creative writing environment

Writing Environment (WE) is a hypertext system being developed at the University of North Carolina to study the writing process. WE was designed around a model of the **cognitive processes**{72} that underlie writing activities. One of the major implications of this model is that a hypertext system should support each phase of the writing process including the development of both content and structure.

WE supports four modes of **authoring**{60} using four separate screen **windows**{9}. A network mode supports the exploratory stage of writing by allowing authors to build free-form networks of ideas. The tree mode supports the synthetic stage of writing by making it easy to study the **hierarchical**{6} relationships among nodes. The editor window is used for the actual writing. The text mode allows the author to see a sequential version of the database as it would appear if it were **printed**{39}.

To facilitate the study of authors using WE, the system includes a tracking capability that records the **path history**{15} of the user. This allows writing sessions to be reconstructed in either real-time or single steps for analysis. See the article by Smith and Weiss about WE in **Hypertext 87 Papers**{139}.

## GUIDE: Hypertext comes to the PC

GUIDE started as a hypertext research project at the University of Canterbury under the leadership of Peter Brown in 1982 to investigate computer display methods. In 1985, Office Workstations Limited (OWL) began to market a version of GUIDE for the Apple Macintosh and subsequently for the IBM PC. The research version of GUIDE runs on a UNIX system.

GUIDE provides three forms of **links**{3}: replacement *buttons*, which replace the activated link with another document (usually an elaboration); note buttons, which produce pop-up windows; and reference buttons, which cause jumps to new documents.

GUIDE was the first hypertext system to be released for personal computers, preceeding Apple's HyperCard by two years. It has been used in a number of commercial Macintosh products including Pagemaker from Aldus and the Savings Zone **product catalog**{25} disk. OWL also markets a **browser**{10} program called the GUIDE Reader — which allows GUIDE databases to be read without the user's having a copy of the GUIDE system — as well as GUIDANCE, a developer's toolkit for creating context-sensitive **help systems**{28}, and the GUIDE Library System, a set of routines that allows GUIDE to be used with **CD-ROM**{15}. In March 1988, OWL announced IDEX, a more advanced version of GUIDE that includes file conversion, **networking**{41}, **security**{50}, and desktop publishing features.

For more information about GUIDE, contact OWL International, Inc., 14218 N.E. 21st St., Bellevue, WA 98007, (206)747-3203. See the article by Brown in **Hypertext 87 Papers**{139}.

## HYPERCARD: Welcome to the stacks

In 1987, Apple Computer introduced the HyperCard program and announced that it would be included free with all new Macintosh computers. By giving HyperCard away, Apple ensures that their version of hypertext is easily available to everyone who buys a Macintosh.

Each document in HyperCard is organized as a set of cards called a *stack*. Each card corresponds to a single screen image. (In traditional **database**{7} terminology, a stack would correspond to a file.) Collections of stacks are called *stackware*.

**Links**{3} between cards are controlled by *buttons*. Buttons can be arrows, icons, words, or shaded areas (See Figure 6.7). When a button is selected with the mouse, a *script* is activated. Scripts can cause a jump to another card, draw a picture, play music or generate speech, access a **CD-ROM**{15} sequence, or launch another Macintosh program. In short, a script is a program attached to a specific node.

The type of **browsing**{10} possible in HyperCard depends upon what kinds of buttons and scripts the stackware developer has provided.

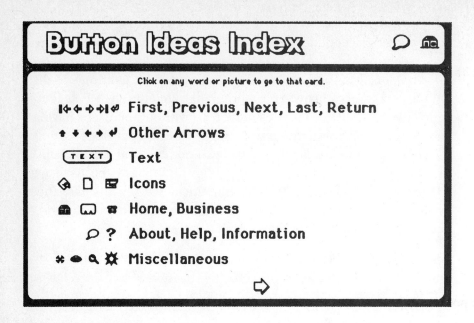

**Figure 6.7** Button Ideas Index screens in HyperCard. (Courtesy of Apple Computer, Inc.)

When you first start a HyperCard stack, you always begin with a Home card that acts as the master index for the stack (see Figure 6.8). HyperCard provides commands to go to the next, previous, first, last, and Home cards in the current stack. There is a "recent" command that shows you miniature displays of the last 42 cards you have seen; you can go directly to any past card by selecting its miniature representation. HyperCard also has a "find text" capability that allows you to search through a stack for the next card containing a specified text string.

HyperCard allows users to create or modify the text or art in a card using built-in **text**{68} and **graphic editors**{69}. It also allows any user to define buttons and the scripts associated with buttons. Scripts are written in a high-level programming language called HyperTalk, which is included with the program. Creating a simple link between cards does not require any explicit HyperTalk programming: HyperCard creates this script automatically. For more about HyperCard, see Goodman (1987) in **References**{137}.

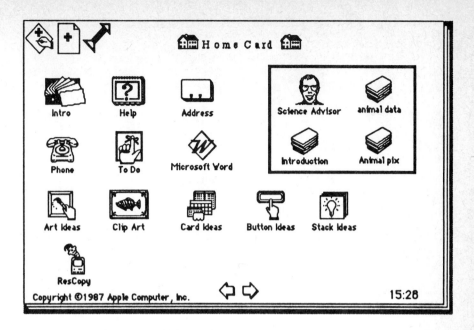

**Figure 6.8** Home Card screen in HyperCard. (Courtesy of Apple Computer, Inc.)

## NAVITEXT: Electronic documentation

NaviText is a program developed by Northern Lights Software Corporation that demonstrates how hypertext can be used for information analysis tasks. NaviText SAM is an online database of the "Human Interface Guidelines" report by Smith and Mosier, which contains over 900 guidelines on **user interface design**{37}.

Using NaviText, it is possible to **browse**{10} through the report selecting specific topics for analysis, to collect and organize guidelines of interest, and to print out a customized report. Figure 6.9 shows an example of an expanded guideline.

Navitext features keyword **searching**{12} and sorting of collected references on the basis of user-supplied ratings. Figure 6.10 shows an example of collected references matching the keyword "respons."

```
═ Table of Contents ═════════════ Line 10 of 25 ═══════════╗
   4   3 SEQUENCE CONTROL
   5   4 USER GUIDANCE
   6      4.0    General
   7      4.1    Status Information
   8      4.2    Routine Feedback
   9         4.2/1            Consistent Feedback
  10         4.2/2    x       Fast Response
  11         4.2/3            Feedback for Control Entries
  12         4.2/4          + Indicating Completion of Processing
  13         4.2/5            Feedback for Print Requests
═ Text Reader ═══════════════════ Line 7 of 15 ═════════════
4.2/2    x       Fast Response

  Ensure that computer response to user entries will be rapid, with
  consistent timing as appropriate for different types of transactions.
Reference
  MS 5.15.1.8
  Shneiderman 1984
     Shneiderman, B. (1984).  Response time and display rate in human
     performance with computers.  Computing Surveys, 16, 265-285.
  Stewart 1980
  See also
1.1/5            Fast Acknowledgement of Entry
▐ Alt-F1 for help  Alt-F10 to exit ▌              ▐ Command: ▌
```

**Figure 6.9**    NaviText SAM screen showing expanded reference. (Courtesy of Northern Lights Software Corp.)

NaviText runs on an IBM PC or compatible. NaviText SAM is designed for software engineers and human factors specialists. For more information, contact Northern Lights Software Corp., 24A Pilgrim Dr., Box 1056, Westford, MA 01886, (508)692-3600.

## BLACK MAGIC: Hypertext word processing

Black Magic is a hypertext word processing program for the IBM PC marketed by NTERGAID. The program provides the usual features of a **text editor**{68} along with hypertext **authoring**{60} capabilities. Three kinds of links can be created in Black Magic: note links that produce pop-up **windows**{9} when activated, reference links that branch to another document, and replacement links that cause one block of text to replace another.

Black Magic allows the integration of graphics with text as well as links to graphics. The program provides a **browser**{10} that shows a graphic

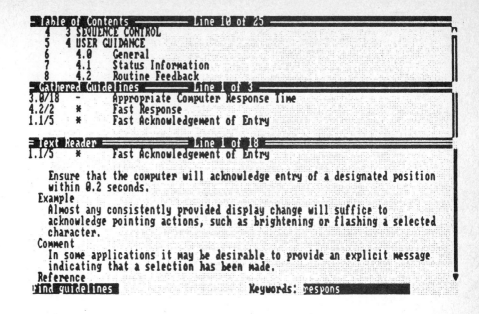

```
─ Table of Contents ─────────── Line 10 of 25 ──────────
   4    3 SEQUENCE CONTROL
   5    4 USER GUIDANCE
   6      4.0    General
   7      4.1    Status Information
   8      4.2    Routine Feedback
─ Gathered Guidelines ─────────── Line 1 of 3 ──────────
3.0/18   -     Appropriate Computer Response Time
4.2/2    *     Fast Response
1.1/5    *     Fast Acknowledgement of Entry
─ Text Reader ─────────────────── Line 1 of 18 ─────────
1.1/5    *     Fast Acknowledgement of Entry

   Ensure that the computer will acknowledge entry of a designated position
   within 0.2 seconds.
   Example
   Almost any consistently provided display change will suffice to
   acknowledge pointing actions, such as brightening or flashing a selected
   character.
   Comment
   In some applications it may be desirable to provide an explicit message
   indicating that a selection has been made.
   Reference
─ Find guidelines ─────────────────── Keywords: respons ──
```

**Figure 6.10**   NaviText SAM screen showing guidelines matching a keyword. (Courtesy of Northern Lights Software Corp.)

representation of all nodes in the database. Black Magic also provides a **bookmark**{14} capability that lets the reader mark return locations.

NTERGAID has made the reader program for Black Magic publicly available. This means that Black Magic documents can be distributed at no cost to the readers. For more information about Black Magic, contact NTERGAID, 955 Connecticut Ave., Bridgeport, CT 06607, (203) 368-0632

## AskSam: Hypertext database manager

AskSam is a **database**{7} management program for the IBM PC from Seaside Software that has been available for a number of years. Version 4.0 adds hypertext capabilities in addition to the standard information retrieval capabilities of a database manager.

AskSam provides a hypertext mode that the user selects from a menu. Once in hypertext mode, the arrow keys are used to select linked terms on the screen. Once a link has been selected, it becomes a standard database query that retrieves all records containing this link. In addition, links can initiate procedures such as printing out a listing or performing a sort. The askSam hypertext system also features a **path history**{15} capability that allows the user to backtrack through earlier choices.

AskSam provides an interesting example of an existing product that has been enhanced by adding hypertext capabilities. It also demonstrates how a hypertext system can benefit from the availability of traditional database management features (or vice versa).

For more information about askSam, contact Seaside Software, Inc., P.O. Box 1428, Perry, FL 32347, (904) 584-8287.

## KnowledgePro: Hypertext expert system

Expert systems are advice-giving systems used to help make decisions or solve problems. They use programming techniques developed in the field of **artificial intelligence**{119} to represent knowledge and make inferences. The "expertise" in an expert system is based upon the knowledge of one or more human experts about a given task or domain.

KnowledgePro from Knowledge Garden, Inc., is an expert system development tool for the IBM PC that includes a hypertext facility. The hypertext capability works like most others; the user selects terms on the screen using the arrow keys. However, in KnowledgePro, the links can be rules that initiate a series of questions to be answered in order for the system to reach a conclusion. Using KnowledgePro, the author has the choice of defining links as associations that result in related information or as decison sequences that clarify or help make a selection.

KnowledgePro is one of the first programs to combine hypertext and artificial intelligence capabilities. Subsequent versions of this program and others are likely to exhibit other interesting features possible with "smart" software.

For more information about KnowledgePro, contact Knowledge Garden, Inc., 473A Malden Bridge Rd., Nassau, N.Y. 12123, (518) 766-3000.

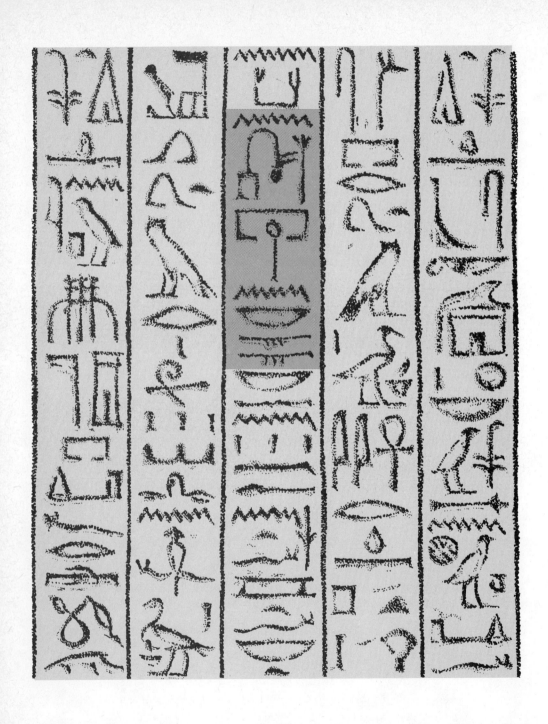

# 7

# Personalities

## OVERVIEW

Like any scientific endeavor, the development of hypertext has been shaped by a small number of prominent researchers. In this chapter we describe some of the key personalities behind hypertext.

The inspired vision of **Vannevar Bush**{99} in 1945 was brought to life by **Doug Engelbart**{101} during the 1960s, while **Ted Nelson**{100} was refining and expanding the theory of hypertext. **Andries van Dam**{102} implemented several early prototypes at Brown University. During the 1980s **Frank Halasz**{103} participated in the NoteCards project at Xerox, while **Ben Shneiderman**{104} developed his interactive encyclopedia system into Hyperties. **Bill Atkinson**'s{101} conception of HyperCard for Apple introduced a hypertext programming language and the appealing graphics of the Macintosh.

Each of these individuals has made significant contributions to the development of hypertext systems and ideas. We think that knowing a little bit about their background and ideas will help you to understand how hypertext has evolved (so far).

## BUSH

In 1945, Vannevar Bush published an article titled "As we may think" in the magazine *Atlantic Monthly*. Bush, a science advisor to President Roosevelt, proposed a major effort to automate technical literature. He described a machine called **MEMEX**{77} that would let an individual **browse**{10} and create a multimedia library of technical documents including personal notes, photographs, and sketches.

Bush had a tremendous vision of the power of hypertext, as he explains in the following excerpt:

> Wholly new forms of encyclopedias will appear, ready-made with a mesh of associative trails running through them, ready to be dropped into the memex and there amplified. The lawyer has at his touch the associated opinions and decisions of his whole experience, and of the experience of friends and authorities. The patent attorney has on call the millions of issued patents, with familiar trails to every point of his client's interest. The physician, puzzled by a patient's reactions, strikes the trail established in studying an earlier similar case, and runs rapidly through analogous case histories, with side references to the classics for the pertinent anatomy and histology. The chemist, struggling with the synthesis of an organic compound, has all the chemical literature before him in his laboratory, with trails following the analogies of compounds, and side trails to their physical and chemical behavior.
>
> The historian, with a vast chronological account of a people, parallels it with a skip trail that stops only on the salient items, and can follow at any time contemporary trails that lead him all over civilization at a particular epoch. There is a new profession of trail blazers, those who find delight in establishing useful trails through the enormous mass of the common record. The inheritance from the master becomes, not only his addition to the world's record, but for his disciples the entire scaffolding by which they were erected. [Bush, 1945, p.108]

We are just beginning to explore the possibilities that Bush envisioned. "As we may think" provided the manifesto for a new way of using computers and organizing information. See Bush (1945) in **References**{137}.

## NELSON

Ted Nelson is one of the ardent champions of hypertext. For the past two decades, Nelson has given countless talks and written many articles about the subject. He invented the term "hypertext" and first described many of the ideas seen in today's hypertext systems.

Nelson was part of the original hypertext group at Brown University. Since 1970, Nelson has been working on his own hypertext system called **Xanadu**{78}, which he envisions as a "universal library" system that allows people to share ideas. His business card lists him as a "computer visionary," and he has described himself as a "computopian" and a "cynical romantic."

In addition to his hypertext evangelism activities and work on Xanadu, Nelson has contributed many new hypertext concepts. For example, he proposed the concept of "stretch text," text that elastically expands or contracts smoothly when selected. He also suggested "hypergrams," a graphics picture in which the components are capable of animation and "perform" when selected.

Nelson has applied his vision of hypertext to many domains, especially learning. In 1970 he published an article entitled "No more teachers' dirty looks. . ." in which he sharply criticized the current ideas about computer-assisted instruction and outlined how hypertext could provide a much better approach:

> Let the student pick what he wishes to study next, decide when he wishes to be tested, and give him a variety of interesting materials, events, and opportunities. . . Under such circumstances, students will actually be interested, motivated to achieve far more than they have ever achieved within the normal instructional framework. . . If they start soon enough they may even reach adulthood with natural minds: driven by enthusiasm and interest, crippled in no areas, eager to learn more, and far smarter than people ordinarily end up being. [Nelson, 1970, p. 21]

Nelson's views are described in his two influential books, *Literary Machines* and *Computer Lib* (see **References**{137}).

# ENGELBART

Douglas Engelbart first started to dream about building hypertext systems in the early 1960s at Stanford Research Institute. In 1968, the first system to exhibit hypertext capabilities, NLS, was publicly demonstrated by Engelbart. NLS was the precursor to the **AUGMENT**{78} system. Engelbart is currently Senior Scientist for Human Augmentation at McDonnell-Douglas.

Engelbart's vision of hypertext involves a system that augments or extends human intellect. He was particularly interested in developing a system that would aid "knowledge workers." Here is how Engelbart described the goal of AUGMENT:

> We recognize explicitly that highly skilled workers in any field, and knowledge work is no exception, are those with a good command of their tools. Our basic design goal was to provide a set of tools that would not themselves limit the capabilities of the people using them. A system designed to encourage more skilled workers will always enable higher human performance than one designed to support less skilled workers. [Engelbart, 1984, p. 465]

Engelbart has concerned himself with all aspects of the work environment including the **user interface**{37} and mechanisms for **collaboration**{49}. He has pioneered many new hardware and software concepts. For example, he was the first to introduce the idea of outline processors as well as the development of software development toolkits. He was also responsible for the development of a five-key handset that allows a user to "chord" input commands. The handset allows the user to enter commands with one hand while moving a mouse (another of Engelbart's contributions) with the other.

# ATKINSON

Bill Atkinson is the primary developer of **HyperCard**{89}. Atkinson is something of a legend in the Apple Macintosh world. He developed the original version of MacPaint, the first **graphics editor**{69} for the Macintosh.

Atkinson has described HyperCard as "a software erector set," that is, a software tool that lets you build other programs. He also has stated that one of the main goals of HyperCard is to encourage people to share information via stacks. Atkinson sees HyperCard as a vehicle that will let more people explore the power of Macintosh computers. In fact, Atkinson insisted that HyperCard be given away free with all new Macintoshes so that it would be available to every Macintosh user.

HyperCard is likely to introduce many people to the idea of hypertext because of its widespread availability. Ironically, its developer didn't set out to create a hypertext system, nor does he think of HyperCard as such. Atkinson is still hard at work on HyperCard, adding new features such as a CD-ROM interface and networking features. It will be interesting to see what direction Atkinson and Apple take with future versions of this influential system — Color? Multiple windows?

## VAN DAM

Andries van Dam has been at Brown University since 1965 and was Chairperson of its Computer Science department from 1979 to 1985. His research has concerned software, computer graphics, text processing, and personal workstations. Much of that research has been on the development of hypertext systems or "computer books" as he refers to them (e.g., **INTERMEDIA**{79}).

In his keynote speech at the **Hypertext 87**{139} conference, (printed in the July 1988 issue of the *Communications of the ACM*, see **References**{137}), van Dam described some of the difficulties he and other hypertext pioneers faced in trying to introduce text-based computer systems:

> When we were doing this work, nobody said "Hey, it's great you're building tools for humanists, that's wonderful, when can we have it?" In fact, it was quite the reverse. Those were the days of accounting on mainframes. . . we really had to fight to get these ideas recognized as legitimate fields of inquiry and to get real users.

Although today we take for granted the use of computers for text processing and graphics, in the early years of hypertext research, computers were seen primarily as numerical machines. Van Dam, however, had a different vision, which he brought to life in a succession of increasingly powerful hypertext systems.

Van Dam has made a number of important contributions to the field of computer science. He was a founder of the ACM special interest group on graphics (SIGGRAPH) as well as the journal, *Computer Graphics and Image Processing*. He also coauthored with James Foley the popular textbook *Fundamentals of Computer Graphics* (Addison-Wesley, 1982).

## HALASZ

Between 1983 and 1986, Frank Halasz worked with Randy Trigg and Tom Moran at the Xerox Palo Alto Research Center to develop the **NoteCards**{82} system. Although the NoteCards system is mainly used within Xerox and a handful of research labs, it has been widely demonstrated and has had a major influence on the design of other hypertext systems.

In 1986, Halasz moved to MCC to work on a project called Hyper-Activity, the application of hypertext ideas to **software engineering**{31}. Halasz, who trained as a psychologist at Stanford, is also interested in the general subject of human–computer interaction and information storage/retrieval.

At the **Hypertext 87**{139} conference, he presented a paper (printed in the July 1988 issue of the *Communications of the ACM*) in which he identified seven issues for the next generation of hypertext systems. The seven issues were:

1. Better search and query capabilities

2. Ability to define collections of nodes and links

3. Virtual structures for dealing with changing information

4. Computation in hypermedia networks

5. Versioning

6. Support for collaboration

7. Extensibility and tailorability

Halasz stated that these issues provide an agenda for future research and development in the hypertext field. In setting out this agenda, he has provided future direction for hypertext systems.

## SHNEIDERMAN

Ben Shneiderman is the head of the Human–Computer Interaction Laboratory and director of the **Hyperties**{86} project at the University of Maryland. He received his Ph.D. in Computer Science from the State University of New York at Stony Brook in 1973 and has been teaching at the University of Maryland since 1976.

Shneiderman's main interests are the design of user interfaces and the experimental study of human–computer interaction. He has written two influential books on the subject, *Software Psychology* (Little, Brown, 1980) and *Designing the User Interface* (Addison-Wesley, 1987) and is the editor of the Ablex series on Human-Computer Interaction.

Shneiderman believes that designers and researchers must go beyond the informal arguments about user friendliness and develop a scientific discipline of user-interface design. He sees hypertext as an easy-to-use yet powerful way of organizing and presenting information. He also feels that there is a need for research on the structure of knowledge and the design of computer systems, in order to take advantage of hypertext.

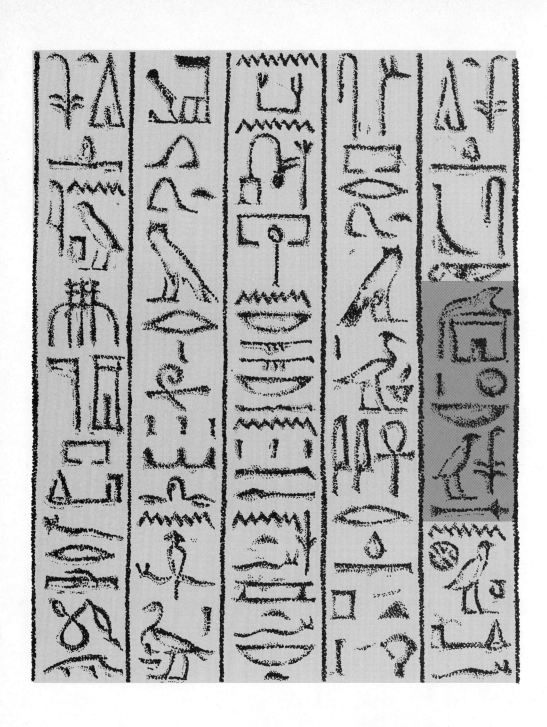

# 8

# Possibilities

## OVERVIEW

This chapter discusses the future prospects for hypertext in business applications such as **job aids**{110} to improve performance, **blueprints**{111} to convey complex details conveniently, and **contracts** {89}, whose complex structures can include references to other documents or legal statutes. **Hyper magazines**{111} or newsletters offer new opportunities for publishing. We also describe provocative personal or home applications such as **cookbooks**{114} that allow links to related recipes, procedures, or descriptions of ingredients, **crossword puzzles**{113} that provide new challenges, and, just for fun, **hyper jokes**{114}. There are other likely applications, such as personal **resumes**{109}, that would enable easy access to major life experiences as well as extensive details, and **travel guides**{109} that can link tourist sites with neighboring hotels, restaurants, or transportation facilities.

The basic theme of this chapter is that we have just begun to explore the possible applications of hypertext. In Chapter 2, a number of applications currently being researched were discussed. In this chapter, we look at some ideas that are no more than that at the moment — ideas on the drawing board.

We also address the **hype**{115} aspect of hypertext. Hypertext is not magic that will automatically produce powerful and elegant computer systems. To truly unlock the tremendous potential of hypertext, the issues introduced in Chapters 3, 4, and 5 must be resolved.

# HYPER TRAVEL GUIDES

With the easy availability of automobile and air travel, we are turning into a world of travellers. There is an ever-increasing need for travel information. *Hypermedia* travel guides offer new possibilities for presenting travel information, including

- combining of print, photographs, and video sequences

- unstructured exploration of topics

- unconstrained size of database

- customization to individual interests

- frequent updating

Each of these potential capabilities addresses limitations of other media currently used to deliver travel information. See the example of a hyper travel guide for San Diego on the *Hypertext Hands-On!* disk.

Related to the idea of hyper travel guides is the idea of using hypertext systems to provide orientations at conferences, airports, corporate lobbies, and shopping malls. Such systems can be engaging and attractive, winning the visitor's attention by the interactivity but maintaining their interest because of the useful and personally chosen information. For example, attendees at a conference can quickly locate sessions, speakers or other attendees, and facilities. Similarly, visitors to a corporate lobby can learn about the organization, locate appropriate departments, or identify specific employees. The **user interface**{37} is particularly critical in public-access situations such as these.

# HYPER RESUMES

Because of the increasing importance of formal qualifications in applying for jobs, resumes are a significant part of the process of job search and selection. One of the difficult aspects of writing or reading a resume is identifying qualifications relevant to a specific job position. Hypertext makes it possible to design resumes in which information is presented at different levels. It is even conceivable that a resume could be in a hypermedia format and include links to actual articles, photographs, or video sequences.

The *Hypertext Hands-On!* disk contains an example of a brief hyper resume for one of the authors.

## HYPER JOB AIDS

Job aids (also called Job Performance Aids or JPAs) are commonly used in technical training to reduce the amount of information that a person needs to know. A typical job aid consists of a list of procedures to be followed. For example, the instructions provided on a pay phone are a job aid; so is the preflight checklist used by a pilot. Hypertext represents an improvement over printed job aids because it makes information easier to find and avoids turning through hundreds of unrelated pages.

For example, the Mitre Corporation is currently exploring hypertext technology for job aids to be used in the NASA Space Station. Due to the complexity of the equipment and procedures involved in operating the Space Station, and the fact that crews will have limited training, job aids will probably play an important role. Hypertext would make it possible for such job aids to contain a large amount of information in a compact form (perhaps using **CD-ROM**{15}) and would make this information easy to find.

Diagnostic problem solving for equipment repair is nicely supported by hypertext because of the high degree of branching required to isolate the source of a failure. Diagnostic and repair procedures can be incorporated into the traversal mechanism. The information obtained using a hypertext repair manual can be made specific to a particular model being repaired and can also be tailored to different skill levels. Hypermedia is especially useful for equipment job aids because diagrams, photographs, and video sequences are often needed.

Of course, there are some limitations to hypertext jol
less portable than paper (unless handheld computers a
puters are subject to damage (they may need to be "rugged
screen readability might not be optimal under all conditions.

## HYPER BLUEPRINTS

Architectural and engineering blueprints have always been a difficult problem for print because they try to represent three-dimensional structures and objects on a two-dimensional surface. Hypertext provides the capability to represent different planes of information as well as three-dimensional graphics.

For example, if you selected a particular section of a building, a full scale blowup of that section would appear. This process could be repeated until the smallest level of detail is reached. Another possibility is that you have the choice of structural diagrams or 3D projections.

There are also exciting possibilities for linking blueprint and **product catalog**{25} hypertext databases. Imagine that you are creating the plans for the bathroom of a new home. You select the bathroom layout from the blueprints and view the sink area. Then you bring up a plumbing supply catalog and peruse the types of faucets available, their dimensions, and their hookup requirements. Perhaps you can use a **graphics editor**{69} to draw a quick sketch of the bathroom with different sink arrangements or maybe even cut them from the catalog and paste them into your sketches.

This scenario is a bit beyond what is possible today. However, there is an example of a simple hyper blueprint on the *Hypertext Hands-On!* disk that illustrates the possibilities described.

## HYPER MAGAZINES

Magazines are an extremely popular form of mass communication. Thousands of magazines cater to every age group and special interest.

Hypertext would allow magazines to go a step farther in their special-ization by providing a customized issue for each subscriber. Readers could essentially make up their own magazine, depending upon which articles or authors they decide to examine. For example, in a gardening magazine, you could link to articles specifically about getting rid of crabgrass or planting fruit trees. In a car magazine, you could select all the links to a specific model of car or feature of interest.

Hyper magazines have several advantages over print:

- Delivery can be more timely.

- New information can be incorporated into existing databases.

- Hierarchical presentation may save reading time.

- Information stored on disk may last longer.

- Search is easier; multiple indexes are possible.

Of course, there are some disadvantages of hyper magazines compared to paper:

- Their portability is limited, and a computer is needed to read them.

- The density of information on a screen is limited.

- It is difficult to reproduce detailed illustrations and photographs.

- There are potential **navigation**{49} problems.

The idea of hyper magazines raises some interesting issues. For one thing, it puts magazine publishers in the database business instead of the printing business. After all, to really take advantage of hypertext capabilities, you need to provide a large selection of material for read-ers to browse through. Hypermedia allows magazines to package print, video sequences, sound, and narrative together in a single form such as **CD-ROM**{15}. This lets magazines (many of which are owned by large entertainment conglomerates) branch into the video, record, and au-diotape domains. Clearly these two issues have strategic importance for the future of **publishing**{55}.

What about advertising? Advertising is the economic force behind almost all magazines — it pays the majority of the costs associated with producing a magazine. In a linear medium such as print (or television), the reader is automatically exposed to ads. However, in a nonlinear medium such as hypertext, it is less clearcut as to where they should be located. Perhaps they could be at the ends of documents or associated with the selection of links so that they appear when the user is jumping from one document to another. Furthermore, ads should allow interested readers to obtain as much (or as little) information about a product as they wish; links to **product catalogs**{25} are desirable. Hypertext opens up a whole new world for advertising!

## HYPER CONTRACTS

In this modern society, we deal with numerous legal documents: real estate contracts, rental agreements, insurance policies, liability releases, business agreements, product disclaimers, and wills. The typical problem with legal documents is that it is hard to understand the major concepts because of the copious detail involved. Hypertext would allow contracts to consist of a lucid **root document**{71} containing the basic concepts with all details to be expanded upon via links. So in addition to reading all the fine print, you would have to check all the links!

One interesting possibility for hyper contracts is to make them sensitive to geographical differences in law. Because laws tend to differ across states (as well as countries and counties), the wording of contracts differs from place to place. A hyper contract could contain the appropriate information for different locales and automatically display the correct wording when the location of the contract is specified. Getting programs to exhibit "intelligent" behavior such as this is one of the goals of **artificial intelligence**{119} work.

## HYPER CROSSWORDS

Doing crossword puzzles of one kind or another is a favorite pastime for many people. Hypertext could be used to link the clues with the appropriate columns and rows. Clues could be longer and include illustrations, sound effects, or spoken narrative. In addition, crosswords could be three-dimensional or multileveled so that each row and column links to other rows or columns.

If you think double acrostics are tough, wait until you try a hyper crossword!

## HYPER JOKES

Jokes are often interesting because they have double meanings. Hypertext would allow a written joke to have many levels of meaning that the reader can link to. Similarly, cartoons could have graphic links that show the thoughts of each character in the cartoon or different humorous outcomes. See the example of a hyper joke on the *Hypertext Hands-On!* disk.

## HYPER COOKBOOKS

Anyone who takes cooking the slightest bit seriously is likely to have a good collection of cookbooks. Cookbooks are similar to **dictionaries**{21}, **encyclopedias**{22}, and **medical texts**{23} in the high degree of cross references involved. A recipe may refer to another recipe for a sauce or pastry required, or it may refer to a discussion of preparation techniques (e.g., how to baste, kneading dough).

In addition to the need for cross references, there is also a need to search for ingredients, equivalents, elaborations, definitions, and serving suggestions. Clearly a hypertext system could provide many advantages over a printed cookbook. A *hypermedia* cookbook would also be able to show photographs and video sequences. And, if we let our imaginations go a little further, how about smell and taste? When you link to the node on Curry Beef, the aroma whaffs from the disk. Just like an electronic version of "scratch and sniff."

# HYPER HYPE?

Enough! By this time, you should be well aware of the vast potential of hypertext to revolutionize information presentation. However, a little perspective is needed on this revolution. First of all, hypertext works only if everyone who wants to use it has easy access to a computer and the appropriate databases are available for sharing (see **public access**{54}). It will likely be some years before most people have such easy access to computers.

Furthermore, somebody has to pay for all of this. **Authoring**{60} a hypertext database requires a tremendous amount of time, and authors will require a reliable method of royalty payment. It took hundreds of years to develop such a system for books, and so we should not expect the intricacies of hypertext **publishing**{55} to get worked out overnight.

Finally, a number of further technological developments are needed in order for hypertext to work smoothly. There are design issues having to do with **screen formats**{64}, **windowing**{9}, **input modes**{65}, **indexing**{11}, and **usability**{37}. There is also the **navigation**{49} problem that sometimes leads to "hyperchaos." **Collaboration**{49} via **networks**{41} remains an area with many open questions. All of these issues will need to be addressed before hypertext systems function satisfactorily.

Hyper promoters and wishful futurists sometimes give the impression that hypertext will bring us nearer to nirvana. Designers who avoid the hype and do the hard work to build substantive hypertext databases and refine the hypertext concept can bring many real benefits to computer users.

Will hypertext realize its full potential? Or is it doomed to be an obscure concept in the annals of computer science? Stay tuned to your computer screen to find out.

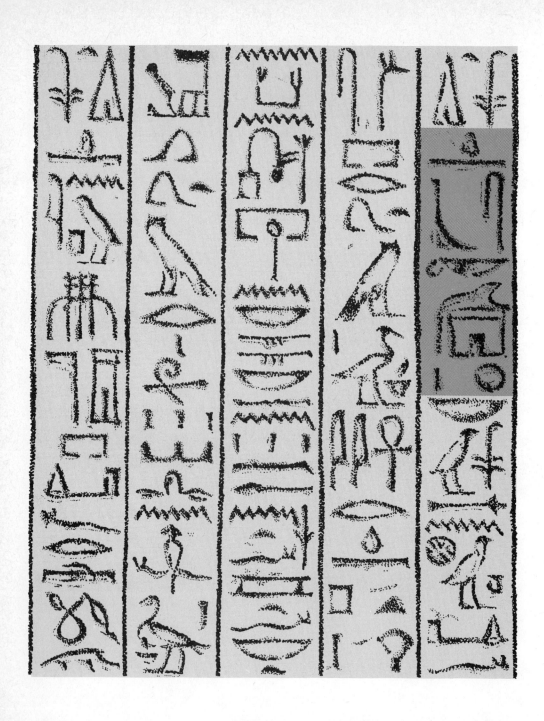

# The End Is Just
# the Beginning

## OVERVIEW

This last chapter discusses the frontiers of hypertext research and practice. It deals with the question: What next? Specific issues discussed include **artificial intelligence**{119}, **user empowerment**{120}, **the role of print**{121}, **business opportunities**{122}, **success factors**{124}, and **getting started**{125}.

# ARTIFICIAL INTELLIGENCE: Making Hypertext Smarter

The goal of artificial intelligence (AI) research is to design "smart" systems that help the user like a competent human assistant. Existing hypertext systems are seen as passive collections of information, but AI workers propose active "agents" that take initiative to guide the reader.

From an AI perspective, the major limitation of current hypertext systems is that they are unable to make inferences about the **links**{3} or the knowledge in the text and graphics contained in the nodes. Thus if nodes A and B are both linked to nodes X, Y, or Z, they probably share one or more things in common. However, hypertext systems do not make this commonality visible to the user. Another simple application would be in a genealogical database. If parent and brother/sister links are included, then the system ought to be able to add grandparent and cousin links automatically.

In an intelligent hypertext system, we might be able to ask questions such as these:

- Are there nodes with further information about Freud's psychoanalytical theory mentioned in the root document?

- Is there a node that contains information that contradicts the historical motivations for the Crimean war as described in the current node?

- Is there an example of the concept of infantilization as presented in the current node?

- How is this node different from the previous node?

- Are there quotes to support the premise that AIDS cannot be transmitted by airborne mechanisms?

Developing a natural language program that could deal with these queries is well beyond the current state of the art. However, if the links in a hypertext database had more semantic information (i.e., contained meaning), if adequately powerful query tools were provided, and if the system contained an inferencing mechanism (programs to produce complex sequences of actions based on stored rules), then it could enable users to pose more complex queries. Such capabilities have been explored by artificial intelligence researchers in various natural-language and expert systems.

Two other important and highly desirable capabilities for hypertext systems also depend on artificial intelligence techniques: "learning" and truth maintenance. Learning refers to the ability of a hypertext database to make generalizations based upon what already exists (produce new links) as well as to identify missing information. For example, the system may note that two concepts seem related but certain information is needed in order to verify this. So with learning capability, a hypertext system might ask its developer a question such as "Hal, should the article on pod bay doors be linked to the one on emergency exit procedures?" Learning might also be applied by having the system record paths that users take and then restructure the links to facilitate frequent paths or to inform users of shortcuts.

Truth maintenance refers to the capability of the system to modify, add, or delete information when new facts are entered. For example, suppose a link points to another link that has become obsolete or has been shown to be incorrect. The system should be able to trace all dependent links and delete/replace them. Truth maintenance also includes the capability to compare two or more links for contradictions and consistency.

Although artificial intelligence techniques can be an inspiration to hypertext designers, much hard work and realistic testing is necessary to bring fantasy into reality. Vague and wishful thinking is useful at early stages of research, but it must lead to precise planning for the software engineering phases. Rigorous testing with users is a powerful stimulus to rapid development of new ideas.

## USER EMPOWERMENT: Putting Users in Control

While artificial intelligence (AI) researchers are trying to develop "smart" machines, there are critics who offer another scenario. User interface (UI) researchers complain that building a sophisticated "intelligent agent" undermines the users' sense of control and their feelings of accomplishment. Instead of designing "intelligence" into the machine, UI researchers seek to empower the user by providing a rich yet comprehensible set of capabilities. Instead of an unpredictable natural-language query facility, UI researchers might develop powerful yet easy-to-use string search with an online thesaurus that could be used to broaden or narrow a search in a user-controlled manner.

Instead of a computer-chosen jump to an unknown node that has been selected by a heuristic program, a UI approach would be to refine techniques for **browsing**{10}, **searching**{12}, or **filters**{13}, and to show comprehensible overviews that highlight nodes based on user actions.

Instead of AI's adaptive machines that magically figure out what the users' needs are and what the users' level of expertise is, UI's adaptable machines enable users to reach their goals by explicitly and easily directing the machine. An adaptable machine would allow users to select the features that they wanted, choose the level of help message desired, and set the density of information displayed.

AI researchers counter these arguments by pointing out that one of the reasons that current computer systems lack usability is because they behave "stupidly." They suggest that even with the most powerful set of user control capabilities, programs unable to make even simple inferences will never be very easy to use. For example, if you make an error, it is desirable for the system to be able to identify the most likely cause(s) of that error; UI proponents would argue that a system should be designed so errors are not possible in the first place.

The debate between AI and UI advocates will undoubtedly heat up in the coming years. You can choose your own vision, joining one of the two camps, or finding a satisfying compromise in the middle ground.

## THE ROLE OF PRINT: Paper versus electronic delivery

One of the goals of *Hypertext Hands-On!* is to demonstrate how the same information differs between printed and hypertext form. If you have tried the disk, you will have realized that the interactivity provided by the computer is the essence of hypertext. However, you may prefer reading the printed version because it is more aesthetically pleasing and more familiar.

With a **display**{37} of better quality than that found on standard IBM PCs, it would be possible to present screens that match the detail of a printed page, including illustrations. Furthermore, the current PC version of Hyperties lacks features that make hypertext more useful, such as **browsers**{10}, **annotation**{41}, and **windows**{9}.

But even with all the possible features, can hypertext replace print? It could, but it probably won't. First of all, the print world has a richly developed infrastructure including school textbooks, publishing and printing companies, libraries, bookstores, and writers. Neither radio nor television managed to supplant print technology; so there is little basis to believe that computer media will.

It is reasonable to believe that hypertext will become a viable alternative to print in those areas in which it offers clear and overwhelming benefits. Many of the applications discussed in Chapter 2 fit this criterion. The key to successful hypertext efforts will be to identify applications in which the unique interactivity of hypertext renders it much more valuable than print.

## BUSINESS OPPORTUNITIES: Making Hyper Bucks

Like any new development in technology, hypertext presents business opportunities for those entrepreneurs who recognize and pursue them. In the preceding chapters, we have briefly discussed some of the potential applications currently being examined, as well as a variety of possibilities.

The first obvious opportunity is selling hypertext systems for different kinds of computers. Many people have brought to the market hypertext systems for personal computers, and we will undoubtedly see many more. Are there big bucks to be made there? Ask the shareholders of Lotus, Microsoft, Aldus, Adobe, or any other company that has ridden the wave of a new category of software for personal computers!

What about mainframes? It seems likely that many of the big companies will eventually want to use hypertext for some of their information retrieval applications. Think of the many government agencies that could use hypertext to find information faster: Social Security, the Veterans Administration, the Department of Motor Vehicles, the IRS (shudder!), not to mention military computer systems. Anyone for a hypertext command and control system?

But maybe the big bucks are to be made in the **databases**{7}. After all, a hypertext system is nothing without a good database. Access to online databases is already a thriving industry—consider Dow Jones, McGraw-Hill, OCLC, or Lockheed's DIALOG. Companies that provide access to databases are in a good position to offer them in hypertext form. On the other hand, there probably will be substantial demand for industry-specific hypertext databases—for the bank, construction, food service, transportation, insurance, communications, or fashion industries.

There are certainly lots of opportunities for single-purpose hypertext programs. For example, consider the U.S. 1040 tax form. With its multiple schedules and attachments, it is ideal for implementation in hypertext form. A number of tax computation programs are already available for personal computers; perhaps they can be married to hypertext systems. Many of the possibilities mentioned in the previous chapter are good candidates for such dedicated programs (such as travel guides, cookbooks, and contracts).

Hypermedia delivered via **CD-ROM**{15} could be a big opportunity, but first people need to buy CD-ROM players. Once they have the player they will want to buy CD-ROM packages. What about the education and home markets? Where will people buy their CD-ROMs? Will CD-ROM dealers become as widespread as videotape stores?

And finally, people will want information about hypertext. So there will be a need for magazines, newsletters, books, courses, and conferences about hypertext, as well as for consultants (hyperexperts).

## SUCCESS FACTORS: Guidelines for managing a hypertext project

Given the large number of potential hypertext applications possible, it is reasonable to predict that many people may become involved in hypertext projects. Here are some guidelines provided by Charles Kreitzberg, president of Cognetics, for successful management of a hypertext project:

1. Build the project around the structuring and presentation of information, not around the technology. Make sure that the structure matches users' needs.

2. Make certain that the project team includes information specialists (trainers, psychologists), content specialists (users, marketers), and technologists (systems analysts, programmers), and that the team members can communicate.

3. Develop a high concept (simple, clear, bold idea) for the body of information you are organizing. Avoid fuzzy thinking when creating the information structure.

4. Keep the navigational structure simple and intuitive. Find a simple, comprehensive, and global structure that the user can easily develop into a cognitive map.

5. Each screen should be self-contained and should not require the user to search his or her memory to understand it or navigate from it. Be sensitive to the possibility that the user will get "lost in hyperspace," and develop the system so recovery is simple.

6. Keep the user's effort very low. Realize that the user is allocating attention among multiple tasks: **navigation**{49}, processing the content of the database, and attending to the business at hand.

7. Users are your best source of feedback; use them throughout the development process to test your designs. Realize that you are not a good judge of your own design because you know too much.

8. Study the target population of users carefully to make certain you know how the system will really be used. Create demonstrations and prototypes early in the project; don't wait for the full technology to be ready.

These recommendations span many of the design, implementation and authoring issues discussed in Chapters 3, 4, and 5. To develop a successful hypertext system, it is necessary to resolve these issues in a fashion that satisfies the above guidelines.

## GETTING STARTED: Your Personal Odyssey

As with any exploration, success is partially determined by the choice of goals. A modest goal would be to study the structure of this or other hypertext documents. You might want to explore other IBM PC systems such as **GUIDE**{88}, **Black Magic**{92}, **askSam**{93}, **KnowledgePro** {94}, or the **NaviText**{91} hyperdocument on "Human Interface Guidelines." The wide availability of **HyperCard**{89} on the Apple Macintosh and its attractive use of graphics and icons makes it an important system to study. Other systems may be harder to view in demonstration form, but they can provide stimulating ideas and examples.

The next step is to try to create your own hypertext document. You might start with something familiar such as your **Hyper Resume**{109}, especially if you already have the contents in computer form. Another modest start would be a personal or family newsletter or family tree in hypertext form. These initial activities will introduce you to the many considerations associated with **authoring**{60} a hypertext database.

More ambitious projects (a day or two of work) might be to implement part of a personnel policy database where you work, a community **Hyper Travel Guide**{109} for your neighborhood (restaurants, stores, emergency services, etc.), or maybe a personal database of your cassette tapes, antiques, or books. These projects would compel you to organize the knowledge in some structured form, recognize relationships within and across groups of **nodes**{5}, identify the central ideas that would become links from the **root document**{71}, and decide how to use **graphics**{67}. You will also become interested in the capabilities of various **authoring tools**{63}.

Once you are satisfied with the modest project you can move on to a major project that might occupy you for several weeks or months. There are many attractive candidates and some of them could become viable commercial ventures. Repair or training manuals, advertisements, corporate annual reports, organization trees for large companies, travel guides, sports and entertainment databases, and self-help guides are all possible. And just for fun, why not try mystery novels, joke disks, and adventure games? Let your imagination be your guide!

At this point you qualify as a fledgling "hyperexpert." Attend a workshop or conference on hypertext, seriously pursue hypertext **business opportunities**{122}, or maybe write your own hyperbook.

# Appendix/Using the Software Version

## OVERVIEW

This appendix discusses the Hyperties component of *Hypertext Hands-On!* To learn how to run the disks, read **Using Your Computer**{127}. To get a general overview of Hyperties, see **About Hyperties on the IBM PC**{132}. **How to browse**{133} discusses browsing strategies for Hyperties. There is also a brief description of the **Hyperties authoring**{134} process (although the Hyperties authoring system is not provided on the disk).

## USING YOUR COMPUTER

The software version of *Hypertext Hands-On!* is contained on the two floppy disks attached to the back cover of this book. To run the software, you will need an IBM PC (or true compatible) with the following equipment:

  1. at least 384K of memory;

2. two 5¼" floppy disk drives, or one 5¼" floppy disk drive and a hard disk;

3. a monochrome or color monitor, and, in order to view the graphics, a CGA, EGA, or VGA graphics adapter.

If you have less than 384K, but more than 256K, you will still be able to use the disks provided, but will not be able to access the SEARCH function. If you have a 3½" floppy disk drive, you can transfer the contents of the two 5¼" disks onto a single 3½" disk (see the note below).

To begin, you must first load DOS—the disk-operating system that comes with your computer. If you are unfamiliar with this procedure, consult your DOS or PC manual, or a knowledgeable friend, before getting started.

Before you do anything with your *Hypertext Hands-On!* disks, you should make backup copies of them. Again, consult your DOS or PC manual if you are unfamiliar with this procedure. Store the original disks in a safe place, and use the backup copies in all the steps that follow.

1. Load the *Hypertext Hands-On!* disks (backups).
   a. If you have two 5¼" floppy disk drives:
      Insert Disk A into the A: drive;
      Insert Disk B into the B: drive.
   b. If you have one 5¼" floppy disk drive and a hard disk:
      Insert Disk A into the A: drive.
   (If you have a 3½" disk drive, see the note below.)

2. Type the following instructions:

   ```
   A: [press the ENTER key]
   HHO [press the ENTER key]
   ```

3. Follow the instructions that appear on your screen. The HHO installation program will guide you through any necessary setup, such as the copying of files to your hard disk or the selection of appropriate colors for your screen display.

Note that Step 3 will occur only the first time you load your disks. After that initial installation, simply type **HHO** [ENTER] and you will go directly into *Hypertext Hands-On!*

4. If you later modify your computer system — for example, change monitors or add a hard disk drive, you will need to change your initial setup. To do this, follow the three steps above, except instead of **HHO** in Step 2, type **SETUP** [ENTER]. Instructions will appear on your screen.

5. The Hyperties system, with which the software version of *Hypertext Hands-On!* has been written, allows you to navigate through the entire work using only the arrow keys and the ENTER key on your keyboard. You may, if you wish, use a mouse to select highlighted items on the screen. However, make sure that your mouse driver is loaded before you begin.

6. To end a session with *Hypertext Hands-On!*, select the following options at any time:

    `EXTRA` [ENTER]

    then select

    `QUIT` [ENTER]

NOTE ON 3½″ FLOPPY DISK DRIVES: If you have one or more 3½″ floppy disk drives (either double density or quad density) and a hard disk, you may want to transfer the contents of *Hypertext Hands-On!* to a 3½″ disk. You will need access to a computer with both a 5¼″ drive and a 3½″ drive. You can transfer the contents of both 5¼″ disks to *one* 3½″ disk by following these steps.

A. Insert Disk B into the 5¼″ drive and a blank, formatted disk into the 3½″ drive.

B. Instruct DOS to access the 5¼″ drive by typing the drive letter, followed by a colon

    `A:` or `B:` [ENTER]

    then

    `COPYHHO` [ENTER]

C. The COPYHHO program will copy the contents of Disk A and Disk B onto the single 3½″ high-density disk (prompting you to change from Disk B to Disk A at the appropriate time). Place this

3½" disk in the A: drive of your own computer when you are ready to run *Hypertext Hands-On!*

Follow Steps 2 and 3 above to run the 3½" version.

## TYPICAL COMPUTER PROBLEMS AND THEIR SOLUTIONS

Computers, like any complex piece of machinery, can have problems from time to time. Sometimes what appears to be an error or problem can be corrected quite simply. Here are several typical situations you might encounter while installing or running *Hypertext Hands-On!*

1. The computer displays:

   ```
   Not ready error reading drive A
   Abort, Retry, Fail?
   ```

   In this case, it is likely that either the disk in drive A: is not seated properly, the drive door is open, the disk is upside down, or there is no disk in the drive. Check the placement of the disk in the drive, re-insert it, close the latch, and type R. If the same message occurs, place a disk you know is good in the drive, close the latch, and type A. If you cannot get the program to load and run, it is possible that you have received a defective disk. See the Important Notes About the Software Version at the beginning of this book.

2. The computer displays:

   ```
   General failure error reading drive A
   Abort, Retry, Fail?
   ```

   It is possible that the disk in drive A: is defective. Make sure it is seated properly, and retry the disk access by pressing R. If the same message is displayed again, place a disk which you know is good in drive A: and press A. See the Important Notes About the Software Version at the beginning of the text for information about obtaining a replacement disk.

3. You are unable to see the difference between standard text and highlighted terms on your computer screen. If this happens, it is

possible that you responded inaccurately to the prompts presented in the Setup program, or somehow bypassed the Setup procedure. Place your backup copy of Disk A in the A: drive, access the A: drive by typing

**A:**[ENTER]

and then type

**SETUP**[ENTER]

The Setup program will help you select the appropriate color set.

4. Your computer will not display any of the graphics in *Hypertext Hands-On!* This means that you either do not have a CGA, EGA, or VGA compatible graphics adapter, or that Hyperties does not recognize your graphics adapter as compatible with one of these standards.

5. The entire program seems to run fine, except that the SEARCH option does not show up on the EXTRA screen. This indicates that your computer has less than 384K of memory. To see the SEARCH function, you must have at least that much memory.

6. You type

**HHO**[ENTER]

and the computer displays:

```
Bad command or file name
```

You apparently have not directed DOS to the drive or directory containing the Hyperties browser. If you are running from a floppy disk, make sure that the correct disk is in the A: drive and that the DOS prompt is "A:." If you are running from the hard disk, you should be in the HHO directory and the DOS prompt should be C:HHO. If it is not, change directories by typing

**C:** [ENTER]
**CD\HHO** [ENTER]

Once you have positioned DOS to be reading from the proper drive and directory, your problem should go away.

If you have a problem not covered above, or the problem persists, see the Important Notes About the Software Version at the beginning of the text.

## ABOUT HYPERTIES ON THE IBM PC

Hyperties consists of two programs: the browser and the authoring system. The **browser**{10} is used to access documents containing text and illustrations in the database. All **links**{3} are highlighted in bold-face. The browser is designed to be very easy to use — only three keys are needed to access any article or illustration: the left and right arrow keys ( <-, -> ) and the ENTER key.

The browser provides an alphabetic **INDEX**{11} of all articles in the database as well as a TABLE OF CONTENTS organized by topics. You can view articles by selecting links or by selecting their titles from the INDEX or TABLE OF CONTENTS. To find titles by their first letters, choose the TURN TO option under INDEX, then scroll over to the first letter and choose that. You can also use the SEARCH feature to **search**{12} through the database for articles containing specific words or phrases that you type in on your keyboard.

When reading an article, you can use the NEXT/BACK PAGE commands to change pages. When you select a link, you may receive a short description of the term at the bottom of the screen. If there is a full article available for the term, you will be given the option to "jump" to that article. If you do jump to another article, you can use the RETURN command to get back to the original article. You can also use the HISTORY feature to see a **path history**{15} of the articles you have already viewed.

The Hyperties **authoring system**{63} is used to create a Hyperties database (you do not have a copy of the authoring system on the disk; it must be purchased separately from Cognetics). To create articles, you can use a built-in **text editor**{68} or any word processing program. Links are indicated by putting tilde marks around terms. The system automatically ties together all linked articles and generates an index for all links created. You can create synonyms for links so that many links jump to the same article. The authoring system also provides a set of formatting commands that can be embedded in the text of an article to control pagination, tabs, margins, and line spacing.

Because of its use of a **direct manipulation**{11} interface using arrow keys or a mouse, the Hyperties system is very easy to use and requires no training. This makes it well-suited for an application such as *Hypertext Hands-On!*

## HOW TO BROWSE

When you first start up your *Hypertext Hands-On!* program, you get the **root document**{71}, which is the Preface to the disk. At this point, you have some choices about how to proceed. You can select a highlighted **link**{3} from the chapter list provided at the end of the Preface, go to the Table of Contents by selecting CONTENTS, or choose the EXTRA option, which will take you to the alphabetic index.

Once you have jumped to another article, you can select another link and jump to a new article, select the INDEX via the EXTRA option, or use the RETURN option to go back to the previous article. If there is a specific topic you want to look for, you can use the SEARCH option to find any article that contains the text string you provide. To perform a search, select EXTRA, go to the INDEX, and choose SEARCH. Your search string can be one word, two words separated by a blank, two words separated by an & to indicate AND, or two words separated by a | to indicate OR.

The path HISTORY feature lets you see a list of all the articles you have viewed in the current session. This is useful if you remember reading something interesting but can't remember which article it was in. To see your path history, select EXTRA and then choose HISTORY from the INDEX.

Online help is available by typing a question mark (?) or pressing CTRL-H. You can use the help to get more information about the options or how to use the browser.

Remember that you can always use the INDEX or CONTENTS to get back to a specific article or to see what else is in the database. There is no "right" or "wrong" way to use a hypertext database, so experiment with different browsing strategies to find the one that is best for you.

## HYPERTIES AUTHORING

Creating an article for Hyperties begins with the step of giving it a title. This title is automatically listed in the index and used to identify the article uniquely. Figure A.1 shows an index screen.

Some of the useful functions provided in the index screen are LINKS, which lists all the links to and from the article selected; SYNONYMS, which lists any synonyms that have been defined for the currently selected article, BROWSE, which lets you invoke the browser so you can see how the selected article looks to the reader, and GRAPHICS, which lists all the graphics currently defined. Once the article is titled, you

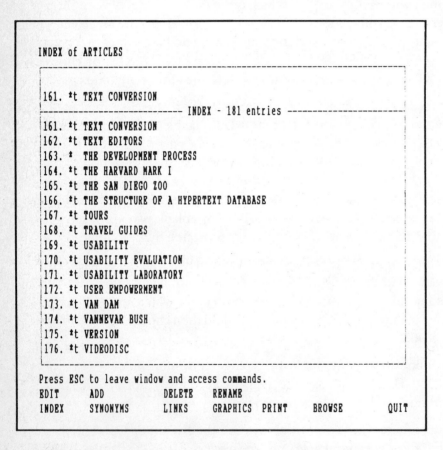

```
INDEX of ARTICLES
-------------------------------------------------------------------
|
| 161. *t TEXT CONVERSION
|------------------------------- INDEX - 181 entries -----------------------|
| 161. *t TEXT CONVERSION
| 162. *t TEXT EDITORS
| 163. *  THE DEVELOPMENT PROCESS
| 164. *t THE HARVARD MARK I
| 165. *t THE SAN DIEGO ZOO
| 166. *t THE STRUCTURE OF A HYPERTEXT DATABASE
| 167. *t TOURS
| 168. *t TRAVEL GUIDES
| 169. *t USABILITY
| 170. *t USABILITY EVALUATION
| 171. *t USABILITY LABORATORY
| 172. *t USER EMPOWERMENT
| 173. *t VAN DAM
| 174. *t VANNEVAR BUSH
| 175. *t VERSION
| 176. *t VIDEODISC
-------------------------------------------------------------------

Press ESC to leave window and access commands.
EDIT      ADD        DELETE    RENAME
INDEX     SYNONYMS    LINKS     GRAPHICS PRINT    BROWSE        QUIT
```

**Figure A.1**   Index screen in Hyperties authoring system. (Courtesy, Cognetics Corp.)

can move to the article screen. Here a heading and definition are provided and the text is entered (or loaded from an existing file). Figure A.2 shows the article screen. **Links**{3} in the text are designated by being surrounded by tilde marks. **Screen formatting**{64} commands are preceded by an @ sign (e.g., @S1 means use single spacing).

Graphics to be included in the articles are created outside of Hyperties using a **graphics editor**{69} that produces ".PCX" files. The author specifies where in the article to show the graphic.

After the articles have been created, an Introductory article (the **root document**{71}) is designated and a title screen can be provided. The Hyperties database is now ready for use.

The Epilog discusses the use of the Hyperties authoring system to create *Hypertext Hands-On!*

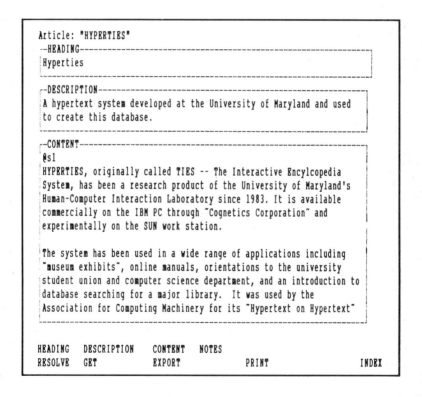

```
Article: "HYPERTIES"
--HEADING-------------------------------------------------------------
Hyperties

-DESCRIPTION---------------------------------------------------------
A hypertext system developed at the University of Maryland and used
to create this database.

-CONTENT-------------------------------------------------------------
@s1
HYPERTIES, originally called TIES -- The Interactive Encylcopedia
System, has been a research product of the University of Maryland's
Human-Computer Interaction Laboratory since 1983. It is available
commercially on the IBM PC through ~Cognetics Corporation~ and
experimentally on the SUN work station.

The system has been used in a wide range of applications including
~museum exhibits~, online manuals, orientations to the university
student union and computer science department, and an introduction to
database searching for a major library.  It was used by the
Association for Computing Machinery for its ~Hypertext on Hypertext~

HEADING    DESCRIPTION    CONTENT    NOTES
RESOLVE    GET            EXPORT              PRINT              INDEX
```

**Figure A.2**    Article screen from Hyperties authoring system. (Courtesy, Cognetics Corp.)

# Bibliography

## REFERENCES

Akscyn, R.N., McCracken, D.M. and Yoder, E.A., "KMS: A distributed hypermedia system for managing knowledge in organizations," *Communications of the ACM,* July 1988, 31 (7).

Ambron, S. and Hooper, K., *Interactive Multimedia*. Redmond, Wash.: Microsoft Press, 1988.

Bly, S. and Rosenberg, J., "A comparison of tiled and overlapping windows." *ACM SIGCHI Proceedings*, Boston, 1986. pp. 101–106.

Brown, C.M., Human–Computer Interface Design Guidelines. Norwood, N.J.: Ablex, 1988.

**Bush**{99}, V., "As we may think." *Atlantic Monthly*, July 1945, 176(1), pp. 101–108.

Conklin, J., "Hypertext: A survey and introduction." *IEEE Computer*, September 1987, 20(9), pp. 17–41.

**Engelbart**{101}, D., "Authorship provisions in AUGMENT." *IEEE Comp-Con Proceedings*, Spring 1984, pp. 465–472.

Frisse, M.E., "Searching for information in a hypertext medical handbook," *Communications of the ACM*, July 1988, 31(7).

Furnas, G.W., Landauer, T.K., Gomez, L.M., and Dumais, S.T., "The vocabulary problem in human–system communication." *Communications of the ACM*, 1987, 30(11), pp. 964–971.

Goodman, D., *The Complete Hypercard Handbook*. New York: Bantam, 1987.

**Halasz**{103}, F., Moran, T.P., and Trigg, R.H., "Notecards in a nutshell." *ACM SIGCHI Proceedings*, Toronto, 1987, pp. 45–52.

Halasz, F.A., "Reflections on NoteCards: Seven issues for the next generation of hypermedia systems," *Communications of the ACM* July 1988, *31(7)*.

Kearsley, G., *Online Help Systems*. Norwood, N.J.: Ablex, 1988.

Kerr, E. and Hiltz, S.R., *Computer Mediated Communication Systems*. New York: Academic Press, 1982.

Lambert, S. and Ropiequet, S., *CD-ROM: The New Papyrus*. Redmond, Wash.: Microsoft Press, 1986.

Marchionini, G. and **Shneiderman**{104}, B., "Finding facts versus browsing knowledge in hypertext systems." *IEEE Computer*, January 1988, 21(1), pp. 70–80.

McCracken, D. and Akscyn, R., "Experience with the ZOG human-computer interface system." *International Journal of Man-Machine Studies*, 1984, 21, pp. 293–310.

Michel, S., "GUIDE—A hypertext solution." *CD-ROM Review*, July/August 1987, pp. 22–24.

Monty, M.L., "Temporal context and memory for notes stored in the computer." *ACM SIGCHI Bulletin*, 1986, 18(2), pp. 50–51.

Monty, M.L. and T.P. Moran., "A longitudinal study of authoring using NoteCards." *ACM SIGCHI Bulletin*, 1986, 18(2), pp. 59–60.

**Nelson**{100}, T., *Computer Lib: You Can and Must Understand Computers Now*. Chicago: Hugos Book Service, 1974.

**Nelson**{100}, T., *Literary Machines*. Swathmore, Pa.: Author, 1981.

**Nelson**{100}, T., "No More Teachers' Dirty Looks." *Computer Decisions*, September 1970, pp. 16–23.

Raymond, D.R. and Tompa, F.W., "Hypertext and the Oxford English Dictionary," *Communications of the ACM*, July 1988, 31(7).

**Shneiderman**{104}, B., "User interface design and evaluation for an electronic encyclopedia." In G. Salvendy (ed.), *Cognitive Engineering in the Design of Human-Computer Interaction and Expert Systems*. Amsterdam: Elsevier, 1987, pp. 207–223.

**Shneiderman**{104}, B., "Designing the User Interface." Reading, Mass.: Addison-Wesley, 1986.

**Shneiderman**{104}, B., "Direct manipulation: A step beyond programming languages." *IEEE Computer*, 1983, 16(8), pp. 57–71.

Tombaugh, J., Lickorish, A., and Wright, P., "Multi-window displays for readers of lengthy texts." *International Journal of Man-Machine Studies*, 1987, 26, pp. 597–615.

Van Dam, A. "Hypertext 87: Keynote Address," *Communications of the ACM*, July 1988, 31(7).

Weyer, S., "The design of a dynamic book for information search." *International Journal of Man-Machine Studies*, 1982, 17, pp. 87–107.

Yankelovich, N., Meyrowitz, N. and **van Dam**{102}, A., "Reading and writing the electronic book." *IEEE Computer*, October 1985, 18(10), pp.15–30.

## HYPERTEXT 87 PAPERS

Hypertext 87 was an invitational conference held at the University of North Carolina, Chapel Hill, November 13–15, 1987. This conference brought together hundreds of people involved or interested in hypertext research. It was the first major conference dedicated solely to the topic of hypertext and as such represents a milestone of sorts in the field of computing. The planning committee for the conference consisted of Frank Halasz (MCC), Mayer Schwartz (Tektronix Corp.), John

B. Smith (UNC), Nichole Yanklelovich (Brown), and Stephen Weiss (UNC). The keynote speakers included **Douglas Engelbart**{101}, **Ted Nelson**{101}, and **Andries van Dam**{102}.

The proceedings from the conference contain 28 papers that cover all aspects of hypertext. In addition, position statements of all participants were published in a separate volume. Six of these papers plus van Dam's keynote address were revised and reprinted in a special issue of the *Communications of the ACM* in July 1988 (indicated by [*CACM*]). Here are the titles of the papers presented:

- "KMS: A distributed hypermedia system for managing knowledge in organizations," R. Akscyn, D. McCracken, and E. Yoder [*CACM*].

- "HAM: A general purpose hypertext abstract machine," B. Campbell and J. Goodman [*CACM*].

- "Turning ideas into products: the guide system," P. Brown.

- "Hypertext and creative writing." J. Bolter and M. Joyce.

- "From the old to the new: Integrating hypertext into traditional scholarship," G. Crane.

- "Searching for information in a hypertext medical handbook," M. Frisse [*CACM*].

- "Hypertext and pluralism: From lineal to nonlineal thinking," W. Beeman et al.

- "Hypertext habitats: experiences of writers in NoteCards." R. Trigg and P. Irish.

- "Comprehending nonlinear text: The role of discourse cues and reading strategies," D. Charney.

- "The notes program: A hypertext application for writing from source text," C. Neuwirth et al.

- "Hypertext and the *New Oxford English Dictionary*," D. Raymond and F. Tompa [*CACM*].

- "Content oriented relations between text units—A structural model for hypertexts," R. Hammwohner and U. Thiel.

- "SuperBook: An automatic tool for information exploration—hypertext?" J. Remde, L. Gomez, and T. Landauer.

- "User interface design for the hyperties electronic encyclopedia," B. Shneiderman.

- "A hypertext writing environment and its cognitive basis," J. Smith, S. Weiss, and G. Ferguson.

- "Constraint-based hypertext for argumentation," P. Smolensky et al.

- "IBIS: A hypertext tool for team design deliberation," J. Conklin and M. Begeman.

- "Exploring representation problems using hypertext," C. Marshall.

- "Thoth II: Hypertext with explicit semantics," G. Collier.

- "The architecture of static hypertexts," T. Oren.

- "Document examiner: Delivery interface for hypertext documents," J. Walker.

- "Hyperworld: One for all and all for one," T. Nelson.

- "The hype in hypertext: A critique," J. Raskin.

- "Relationally encoded links and the rhetoric of hypertext," G. Landow.

- "Reflections on NoteCards: Seven issues for the next generation of hypertext systems," F. Halasz [CACM].

- "Developing and distributing hypertext tools: Legal inputs and parameters," H. Jones, III, Esq.

- "Abstraction mechanisms in hypertext," P. Garg [CACM].

- "Manipulating source code in dynamic design," J. Bigelow and V. Riley.

- "On designing intelligent hypertext systems for information management in software engineering," P. Garg and W. Scacchi.

The Hypertext 87 Proceeedings are available from the Department of Computer Science, University of North Carolina, Chapel Hill, N.C. 27599-3175. A second report on the conference, Hypertext 87 Digest, is available for the Macintosh from Eastgate Systems, Inc., P.O. Box 1307, Cambridge, Mass. 02238.

In addition to the printed proceedings and articles, the conference material has also been made available in hypertext form. Two versions of the papers published in the CACM are available, one using **Hyperties**{86} developed at the University of Maryland, and one using **HyperCard**{89}, created by a team at Brown University. These disks are both available from ACM Headquarters, 11 West 42nd St., New York, N.Y. 10036. A HyperCard trip report of the conference was created by Jakob Nielsen of the Technical University of Denmark. Figure B.1 shows the title screen, topic map, and a notes page from Nielsen's report.

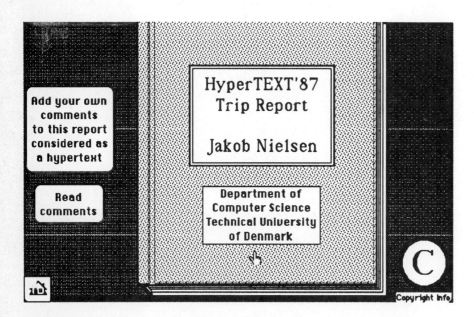

**Figure B.1**    Screens from HyperCard trip report by Jakob Nielsen. (Reproduced with permission of the author.)

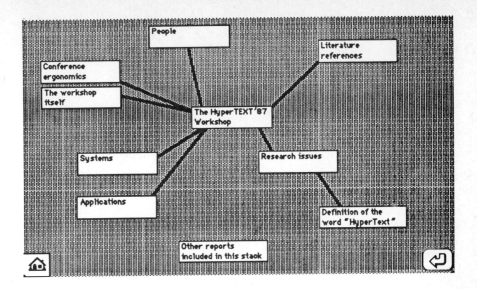

HyperTEXT '87 took place in Chapel Hill, North Carolina November 13-15, 1987 and was the first large-scale meeting devoted to the hypertext concept. Before the workshop, hypertext had been considered a somewhat esoteric concept of interest to a few fanatics only. So just in case some readers don't know what hypertext is, here is a button to click on if you want to read my definition:

## Definition

Towards the end of the workshop there was considerable talk of making the proceedings and the position papers available as a hypertext document. Doing so would of course be in the spirit of the workshop theme and there is some chance that it may be done. On the other hand, there are also several problems with such issues as what kinds of links would be made between documents. It is not clear that a given author would like to see specific links into and/or out from his/her paper, as the presence (or even absence) of the links could change its interpretation.

Hypertext (abbreviated HT in most of this report) has seen considerable interest recently because of some new commercial hypertext products such as Guide from Owl and HyperCard from Apple running on popular personal computers such as Macintosh and IBM. When the workshop was originally planned in the fall of 1986, the planners were not sure whether they would be able to get a large enough set of papers and participants.

But they had ended up having 500 people compete for the 200 seats at the workshop. At the end of the workshop, Ted Nelson compared it to the first SIGGRAPH conference on interactive computer graphics. It had also had a small and cosy feel but now it was a gigantic conference with 30,000 people. Nelson felt that HT would also grow to be an industry.

( Conference Ergonomics )

Add your own comment          Read comments

# HUMAN FACTORS RESEARCH

There is a tremendous interest in hypertext's human interface from such disciplines as computer science, library science, communications, and business. The Hypertext 87 conference was an important event, but there are many other sources of information. The Association for Computing Machinery (ACM) has a Special Interest Group on Computer and Human Interaction (SIGCHI), which publishes a quarterly newsletter and holds regularly scheduled conferences whose proceedings are an especially valuable resource. The ACM's Special Interest Group on Office Information Systems (SIGOIS) also covers hypertext systems.

The American Society for Information Science (ASIS) has a Special Interest Group on User Online Interaction (SIGUOI), which publishes a quarterly newsletter and participates by organizing sessions at the annual ASIS convention. The International Federation for Information Processing Societies (IFIPS) has a working group WG 6.3 on human-computer interaction, which publishes a quarterly newsletter called *Interact*. The Human Factors Society also has a Computer Systems Group with a quarterly newsletter.

Conferences, such as the ones held by the Association for Computing Machinery (ACM), Special Interest Groups on Computer–Human Interaction (SIGCHI) and Graphics (SIGGRAPH), American Society for Information Science (ASIS), Human Factors Society, and IFIPS, often have relevant papers presented and published in the proceedings.

Journals in which you are likely to find papers about hypertext and the user interface issues include:

*ACM Computing Surveys*

*ACM Transactions on Office Information Systems*

*Behaviour and Information Technology (BIT)*

*Communications of the ACM (CACM)*

*Ergonomics*

*Human Factors (HF)*

*IBM Systems Journal*

*IEEE Computer*

*IEEE Computer Graphics and Applications*

*IEEE Transactions on Systems, Man, and Cybernetics (IEEE SMC)*

*International Journal of Human–Computer Interaction (IJHCI)*

*International Journal of Man-Machine Studies (IJMMS)*

# Epilog/
# The Making of
# *Hypertext*
# *Hands-On!*

One of our interests in developing *Hypertext Hands-On!* was to compare the relative virtues of print and electronic information delivery. We were curious to see how different aspects of hypertext would work in printed format. The idea of using hypertext to explain itself was intriguing.

Our first challenge was how to show **links**{3} on the printed page. Putting the linked terms in boldface seemed to be the equivalent of highlighting them on the disk, but how could they be activated? Putting the page number of the linked nodes directly after the link seemed the closest we could come to a direct "jump" to that node.

In Hyperties, a definition is provided when you select a link. This gives you a chance to get a little more detail about the link without jumping to it. To replicate this feature in the book, we tried putting definitions of the linked terms in small print at the end of each article. However, this made the pages very cluttered, and a lot of the definitions were redundant, especially for common links. So we dropped the definitions from the body of the text and moved them to the glossary.

Another major challenge was sequencing of material in the book. On the disk, the order of the articles doesn't matter because they are accessed and stored in a random fashion. However, in the book, the articles had to follow some logical order. This lead to the development of traditional chapters based on topics. However, within the chapters, the order of articles was basically arbitrary. Because each article was written as a self-contained "chunk" with both forward and backward links, there was no obvious sequence of articles.

One thing we realized quite early was that the book and the disk would have quite different types of illustrations. For example, we could show detailed screen shots in print that we could not do on the disk because of the relatively low resolution of the standard color **display**{37} on the IBM PC. On the other hand, we could present color **graphics**{67} on the screen that would be expensive to do in print.

When early versions of the book and disk were reviewed, we discovered that readers found the short articles in the book choppy and many of the articles on the disk too long. This made us realize that the book needed to have larger articles, whereas the disk needed even shorter articles. In addition, the book needed to have more structure and integration because it was being read in a linear fashion.

From this experience, we reaffirmed what we already suspected, namely, that hypertext is best suited to presenting information that has a complex linked structure and is not suited for presenting strongly sequential information. Actually, we found out something even more interesting: Even when the information does not have any real structure, readers demand structure in a book (unless it is explicitly identified as a nonstructured document such as a catalog or newsletter). We had to create a sequential structure for the print version of *Hypertext Hands-On!* that was not needed for the software version.

# THE DEVELOPMENT PROCESS

*Hypertext Hands-On!* took about five months to create. We began by writing the initial drafts of articles as ASCII files. These files were then loaded into XyWrite for production of the book version and into the Hyperties authoring system for the disk version. The XyWrite versions were then formatted as pages with specific type styles and sizes, line spacing, and page widths. The Hyperties versions were linked and formatted properly for screen displays. At this point, the same information existed in two different forms. Although the content was the same, the formatting codes that had been added to the files were quite different for print and screen layout.

The Hyperties authoring system has a number of features that help the author manage the incremental development process. For example, it provides a list of all the article titles that have been referenced and marks the ones that have already been created. Overall, the Hyperties strategy of requiring articles to have titles was a positive stimulus to helping us organize the manuscript and to adding links conveniently (it is also a great aid during browsing). The capability to create synonyms for articles enabled us to use varied terms to link to the same article. A great time saver is the fact that once a term is linked to an article, future marked occurrences of the term are linked automatically.

With the initial version of the book and disk complete, we started the review process. As we got new ideas and feedback on existing articles, we added and revised text. New information could be created as ASCII text files and loaded directly into the XyWrite files as appropriate. However, the initial version of the Hyperties authoring system did not allow text files to be inserted into existing files (you could only load new files). To get around this limitation, it was necessary to load the existing Hyperties files into XyWrite (any **text editor**{68} would have worked), make the insertion of the new file and save it, go back to Hyperties, delete the original article, and finally load the revised article as a new file. Needless to say, the capability to insert new files into existing articles became a high-priority addition to the Hyperties authoring system. This is a good example of a feature whose need was not apparent until the system was used in a long-term development effort where substantial revision was involved.

Another revision problem had to do with changes to the **links**{3}. It was not uncommon to modify a link name or decide to delete it. The citation feature of Hyperties lists all the references from and to an article and hence could be used to identify where the changes were needed. However, each link had to be changed manually by editing the article it was contained in. As the number of articles increased, this became very tedious.

An additional difficulty that arose during the revision process was how to identify changes to the disk version. With the paper version, reviewers could make annotations in the margins. But Hyperties has no **annotation**{41} capability. So reviewers would make a screen print and annotate this or write a description of the location such as "second screen of the article on displays, third paragraph." Although both of these techniques worked, it required more effort on the part of the reviewers than if they could have made their remarks directly in a comment window or a note tied to a specific screen location.

A final problem that emerged during the development process was the space limitation of a single 5¼ inch floppy disk. As the number of text files started to grow large and we started to add more graphics, it quickly became apparent that we could not fit the entire database on one disk, even though all of the files would be stored in a compressed format developed by Cognetics. A single 3½ inch disk would have accommodated our needs, but we knew that most people still have the older disk drives. So we decided to provide two floppy disks. This required changes to the Hyperties system as well as additional information in the Using Hyperties section on how to use the program.

Almost all of these problems have to do with the limitations of the original Hyperties authoring system. More powerful **printing**{39} capabilities might have eliminated or reduced our need to use a separate text editing program and work with two different sets of files. Searching, bidirectional links, and annotation capabilities would have made the revision process easier. On the other hand, the simplicity and ease of use of the Hyperties authoring system made it possible to create the *Hypertext Hands-On!* disk very quickly and without any significant learning time.

# WHAT THE REVIEWERS SAID

Writing a book is always a learning experience. A lot of that learning comes from comments and feedback provided by reviewers. We were fortunate to have a number of reviewers of the initial draft of *Hypertext Hands-On!* (including an entire class of a Hypertext seminar conducted at the University of Maryland). Here are some of their remarks:

> What I value most of the Hands-On program and Hyperties is the use of embedded menus, because people tend to think in terms of relationships instead of options. Regular menus and indexes provide all the facts, but they don't provide a means to relate one thing to another.

> The linking mechanism employed in this hyper book frees the reader of the author's conceptions regarding the holistic relationships of the facts, which in turn forces the reader to become a contributing author or at least an editor in realtime. . . Interesting.

> *Hypertext Hands-On!* seems to provide a thorough introduction to the emerging field of hypertext. However, I prefer the book form over the software version. One reason for this preference is my desire to know I have seen everything in the software version. The only way to do this is to go through the index, keeping track in my head.

> I found *Hypertext Hands-On!* fascinating and pleasantly addictive. I appreciated the effort to keep the articles short. This permitted me to cover many different topics in a small amount of time.

> In spite of the obvious best intentions of the authors, the product seems like an advertisement for everything that is wrong with hypertext as a technology. The fundamental problem is that they have let the discrete nature of hypertext drive the material, rather than having the content of the material drive the presentation. They have tried to parse all the ideas, functions, definitions, people, activities, problems, and descriptions into equal-sized pieces that could be retrieved randomly. The result is a disorganized jumble of topics.

> I am personally excited about hypertext and its relatives as a source of ideas for user interface, means of interpersonal communications, and an approach to dealing with large amounts of data. I think, though, that these ideas must prove themselves; I don't take their virtues on faith.

> Education in general, and computers in specific, have up until now rewarded linear/logical thinking. Hypertext, however, changes that by encouraging intuitive cognition.

A nice overview of hypertext that is highly readable. . . I think that designers/programmers can benefit by the clear and clever language and style, and the general reader can gain a good entry into what hypertext is all about.

I guess I'm not sure who the audience is. I suppose the book could be included in an education course on computers, an introductory course on computers, or a training course.

To succeed, *Hypertext Hands-On!* should be both a good book and a good hyperbook. It is not. As a book, it is hobbled by having to fit into the hypertext style. . . As a program relegated to the least common denominator of personal computers, it lacks what is good about books — illustrations, visible structure, and easy reading.

Many people had problems with our initial choice of links — they complained that there were too many, that the names were not always meaningful in terms of what they linked to, and that the synonyms were frequently confusing because it was not immediately apparent what the relationship between the synonym and the original link was. So we reduced the number of links, tried to choose better names, and clarified the synonyms.

Some people wanted changes in the way the backtracking worked in Hyperties. They wanted more graphics (we obliged). We had some incorrect links to fix (e.g., selecting the link "medical textbooks" brought up "performance issues"). Everybody wanted more depth, more discussion, more detail. What a thirst for knowledge! And everybody hated our original **hyper joke**{114} about a bar fly. So we replaced it with something more subtle.

Incidentally, it's interesting to observe that if Hyperties had annotation capability, we could have distributed the *Hypertext Hands-On!* disk with the reviewers comments on the disk. So using the program would be like participating in a group conversation instead of a monolog.

After many revisions and improvements to the software (a final round of reviews and usability tests with dozens of students and professionals), we made further changes in the interface and format (sped-up retrieval and further compaction to permit more graphics) and in the contents (copyediting, updated references, etc.). We learned a lot, and we hope you will too!

# COLLABORATION AT A DISTANCE

Because the authors of *Hypertext Hands-On!* live on opposite sides of the country, almost all of the **collaboration**{49} was done via telephone or exchange of material via mail (overnight courier services when we were in a hurry). We also used an **electronic message**{73} system (MCI Mail) to discuss the project and exchange files.

We could have done all of our collaboration online but we didn't. Why? Put simply, there was really no need to. Because the project took place over a long enough period of time, mail was sufficiently fast. We also needed to exchange many documents about hypertext that were in printed form. The telephone provided an interactive medium that allowed us to discuss ideas — something that doesn't work as well when stretched out over a series of electronic mail messages.

Another consideration that favored traditional communication channels was the fact that there were just two authors. If the project had involved a larger group of authors, it might have been more beneficial to use an online network due to the logistical problems of trying to arrange conference calls or to send multiple copies of manuscripts and files to people in different places. Actually, interaction wth our editor at Addison-Wesley, Peter Gordon, who was heavily involved in all aspects of the project, did become complicated at times — suggesting that once the number of collaborators goes to three or more, online networks start to have a strong advantage.

Detailed discussions of the book were easy to do because we could easily look at our copies of the manuscript (which we all carried with us on various trips), but detailed discussion of the disk was more difficult. Although both authors have easy access to PCs, they were not always handy when the phone rang. The capability to access Hyperties on a network and to be able to send messages in real time while viewing screens would facilitate this type of discussion. In lieu of real-time messaging (or in addition to it), annotation capability would be useful.

To summarize, traditional forms of communication (i.e., telephone and mail) met our needs in collaborating on this project. Had the timeframe been shorter or had there been more authors, the use of networks might have been preferable. Furthermore, if Hyperties could operate over a telecommunications network, online collaboration would have been much more likely.

## THE ONLY THING THAT DOESN'T CHANGE IS CHANGE ITSELF

Neither the subject of Hypertext nor the Hyperties system will stay the same for very long. In addition, the personal computer field makes tremendous advances every few years. Thus, we anticipate being able to develop new editions of *Hypertext Hands-On!* that will include more information about hypertext, take advantage of new capabilities added to Hyperties, and use additional features of personal computers. Many new hypertext design ideas, applications, and systems are likely appear in the next year or two. Additional capabilities (e.g., **windows**{9}, graphical **browsers**{10}, **filters**{13}, **bookmarks**{14}, **annotation**{41}) will likely be added to the PC version of Hyperties. As more and more people buy PS/2 type machines, higher resolution graphics will be possible, along with more storage space and speed.

If you found this first version of *Hypertext Hands-On!* interesting, we're sure you will love the sequel. Coming soon to your favorite book or computer store!

# Hyper Glossary

This glossary provides a brief explanation of important terms and brief definitions of the links contained in the book. It can be used as an alphabetical index to the linked terms; the page number of the link is provided in brackets.

**Aliasing**{43}: The technique of allowing multiple synonyms for the same node or command.

**Annotation**{41}: The capability of users to make additions to a hypertext document.

**Artificial intelligence**{119}: Field of computer science that concerns itself with the design of programs that can reason and solve problems.

**ASCII**: A standard file format for IBM Personal Computers (American Standard Code for Information Interchange).

**askSam**{93}: A database program for personal computers with hypertext capabilities.

**Atkinson, Bill**{101}: Developer of HyperCard.

**Augment**{78}: One of the oldest operational hypertext systems (originally called NLS).

**Authoring**{60}: The process of creating hypertext documents.

| | |
|---|---|
| **Authoring principles**{62}: | Guidelines for the creation of hypertext documents and databases. |
| **Authoring tools**{63}: | A program used to create a hypertext database. |
| **Bit-mapped**: | A type of graphic in which every single element can be addressed (contrast with Object-oriented). |
| **Black Magic**{92}: | A hypertext word processing program for personal computers. |
| **Blueprints**{111}: | Hypergraphics used to show multiple levels of architectural or engineering drawings. |
| **Bookmarks**{14}: | A location marker placed by the user. |
| **Browsing**{10}: | Exploring a hypertext database by following links. |
| **Bush, Vannevar**{99}: | The first person to describe the idea of hypertext. Bush called his system MEMEX. |
| **Business opportunities**{122}: | Hypertext opens up new business possibilities including systems, databases, and CD-ROMs. |
| **Buttons**: | The name given to icons or symbols used to designate a link. |
| **CD-ROM**{15}: | A standard for high-density storage using optical disks (Compact Disk-Read Only Memory). |
| **Cognitive processes**{72}: | Strategies for solving problems, learning and understanding. It is frequently argued that hypertext functions in the same manner as we think. |
| **Collaboration**{49}: | Multiple authoring of hypertext databases. |
| **Compatibility**{52}: | The ability to share hypertext databases across different computer systems. |
| **Contracts**{113}: | Hypertext can make contracts and other legal documents easier to understand by hiding the detail until it is needed. |
| **Cookbooks**{114}: | Hypertext could make it easier to cross reference information for recipes, ingredients, techniques, and meal planning. |

**Creative writing{27}:** Hypertext can be used as a medium to promote new writing strategies.

**Crosswords{113}:** Hypertext can provide multilevel puzzles and games.

**Databases{7}:** Organized collections of information.

**Default:** The standard setting or value used if a different one is not provided or selected by the user.

**Dictionaries{21}:** A natural application for hypertext because of the many cross references to word definitions.

**Digitizing:** Converting a printed image or text into electronic form (also referred to as scanning).

**Direct manipulation{11}:** The use of pointing for input via touch, mouse, or arrow keys.

**Displays{37}:** The resolution and size of a display monitor affects the usability of a hypertext system.

**Document size{71}:** Research studies suggest that shorter documents are easier to understand in a hypertext database.

**Electronic messaging{73}:** Use of an online network for sending mail and conducting conferences.

**Encyclopedias{22}:** A good application for hypertext due to the rich cross references possible.

**Engelbart, Douglas{101}:** A hypertext pioneer and developer of the Augment/NLS system.

**Filters{13}:** Functions that allow hypertext users to restrict the information displayed.

**Fisheye views{43}:** Changing the amount of information displayed depending upon its proximity to the current location.

**Getting started{125}:** Try out some of the hypertext systems and attempt to create simple databases in your area(s) of expertise or interest.

**Graphics{67}:** All nontextual information in a hypertext database.

| | |
|---|---|
| **Graphics editor**{69}: | Lets you create and modify electronic art. |
| **GUIDE**{88}: | One of the first hypertext systems available for personal computers. |
| **Halasz, Frank**{103}: | One of the primary developers of the Xerox NoteCards system. |
| **Help systems**{28}: | Facilities that provide users with online assistance. |
| **Hierarchical views**{45}: | Displaying different levels in a hypertext database that is structured as a hierarchy. |
| **Hierarchies**{6}: | In a hierarchy, nodes and links are arranged in a tree structure. |
| **Hype**{115}: | Unsubstantiated claims or unrealistic expectations about what hypertext is and what it can do. |
| **HyperCard**{89}: | The hypertext system marketed by Apple Computer for the Macintosh. |
| **Hypermedia**: | A hypertext database consisting of different types of information (e.g., text, photographs, sound/speech, video). |
| **Hypertext**{3}: | Nonlinear organization of information. |
| **Hyperties**{86}: | The hypertext system developed at the University of Maryland and used for the *Hypertext Hands-On!* disk. |
| **Icons**: | Graphic symbols that represent actions or files. |
| **Indexing**{11}: | An organized set of links to facilitate searching of hypertext databases and to improve navigation. |
| **Input modes**{65}: | The use of a keyboard, mouse, touch screen, or graphics tablet to input information to a hypertext system. |
| **Instruction**{30}: | Hypertext provides for new forms of interactive learning and teaching. |
| **Integration**{42}: | The capability to transfer information from a hypertext program to other application software. |
| **Intermedia**{79}: | A hypermedia system developed at Brown University. |
| **Job aids**{110}: | The use of hypertext to provide online job assistance. |
| **Jokes**{114}: | Hypertext can be used to present multiple levels of humor. |

**KMS**{83}: The Knowledge Management System is a hypertext system primarily designed for multi-user problem solving.

**KnowledgePro** {94}: An expert system with hypertext capabilities for personal computers.

**Links**{3}: Connections between one document and another.

**LISP**: A computer language widely used for artificial intelligence applications.

**Magazines**{111}: Hypertext magazines allow readers to browse through articles in a richer fashion than do existing printed magazines.

**Medical textbooks**{23}: Medical knowledge is well suited to hypertext databases because of the many interrelationships.

**Megabyte**: One million bytes. A byte is the basic unit of digital storage and is equivalent to one character or eight bits of information.

**MEMEX**{77}: The first hypertext system, envisioned by Vannevar Bush.

**Museum exhibits**{33}: Hypertext databases allow vistors to personalize exhibits to their own interests and depth of knowledge.

**Navigation**{49}: One of the major issues in using hypertext is navigating around the database without getting lost or confused.

**Navitext**{91}: A hypertext database system for IBM PCs developed by Northern Lights Software.

**Nelson, Ted**{100}: One of the pioneers of the hypertext field and developer of the Xanadu system.

**Neptune**{86}: A multilevel hypertext system developed by Tektronix.

**Networks**{41}: Computer systems linked via local cabling or telecommunications.

**Node**{5}: The smallest unit of information in a hypertext database to which a link can be made.

**NoteCards**{82}: A hypertext system developed for Xerox LISP workstations.

**Object-oriented**: A type of graphic that is composed of separate components called objects (contrasts with Bit-mapped).

| | |
|---|---|
| **Packet switching**: | A telecommunications strategy in which information is transmitted in small units, each of which has a destination address for a computer in a network. |
| **Path history**{15}: | A trace of all actions that allows you to back up to previous documents. |
| **Performance**{39}: | The amount of time it takes a hypertext system to respond to a user. |
| **Pixel**: | The smallest addressable point on a display. Abbreviation for picture element. |
| **Print**{121}: | Print has some important advantages over hypertext: portability, lower costs, and familiarity. |
| **Printing**{39}: | Printing of hypertext documents raises a variety of formatting issues. |
| **Product catalogs**{25}: | Hypertext is ideal for catalogs because of the many cross references involved. |
| **Public access**{54}: | The availability of hypertext systems and databases to the public. |
| **Publishing**{55}: | Dissemination of hypertext documents. |
| **Record**: | The name given to a single collection of fields in a database. |
| **Religious studies**{32}: | Hypertext is useful for religious studies because of the many explanations involved. |
| **Resumes**{109}: | Hypertext can be used to present multiple views of an individual. |
| **Rights**{53}: | Hypertext introduces new legal issues for copyright, liability, and contracts. |
| **Root document**{71}: | The initial document a reader sees in a hypertext database. |
| **Screen formats**{64}: | Some of the major issues in designing screens include spacing, scrolling, and windowing. |
| **Script**: | A program that defines how a link works when activated. |
| **Searching**{12}: | The capability to find information via keyword matches is an important feature that should be available in hypertext systems. |

**Security**{50}:      Controlling access in multiuser systems.

**Shneiderman, Ben**{104}:      Developer of the Hyperties system. Head of the Human-Computer Interaction Lab at the University of Maryland.

**SMALLTALK**:      A computer language in which all entities are treated as objects that can send messages to each other.

**Software engineering**{31}:      Programming is a good application for hypertext because of the many interrelationships involved in programs.

**Sound/ speech**{68}:      Synthesized speech and sound are important aspects of hypermedia.

**Stack**:      The name Apple Computer gave to HyperCard documents.

**Stackware**:      A collection of stacks (HyperCard documents).

**Structuring hyper- knowledge**{61}:      The relationships among concepts in a hypertext database must be explicitly identified.

**Success factors**{124}:      Successful design and implementation of a hypertext system depends upon matching system, user, and organizational factors.

**Technical documen- tation**{29}:      Hypertext is well suited to technical documents because it allows the reader to focus on the relevant information.

**Text conversion**{51}:      The challenge of converting print documents to electronic form for inclusion in hypertext databases.

**Text editors**{68}:      Software that allows the creation and modification of hypertext and other documents.

**Tiling**:      Windows that cover the entire display screen and do not overlap.

**Tours**{14}:      Prespecified paths through a hypertext database.

**Travel guides**{109}:      Hypermedia has considerable potential for presenting travel information in random-access fashion.

**Usability evaluation**{56}:      More objective and precise means of measuring user satisfaction with hypertext systems are needed.

| | |
|---|---|
| **Usability/user interface**{37}: | How easy or hard it is to use a hypertext system. |
| **User empowerment**{120}: | Giving users more control of a hypertext system is likely to make the system more useful and powerful. |
| **UNIX**: | An operating system originally developed at Bell Labs. |
| **van Dam, Andries**{102}: | A hypertext pioneer responsible for much of the work at Brown University. |
| **Versions**{40}: | Keeping track of different versions of hypertext documents is a complex problem. |
| **WE**{88}: | A hypertext system developed at the University of North Carolina designed to facilitate creative writing. |
| **Webs**: | A group of links that share the same attributes. |
| **Windows**{9}: | Allow the screen to be divided into separate display areas. |
| **WYSIWYG (What You See Is What You Get)**: | Capability to print things exactly as they appear on the screen. |
| **Xanadu**{78}: | The hypertext system developed by Ted Nelson. |

# Index

This index is for the book version of *Hypertext Hands-On!* On the disk version you can use the powerful SEARCH feature to locate all occurrences of a word or pair of words.

ACM, 102, 144
adventure game, 25
advertising, 113
airports, 109
AIRS, Inc., 32
alphabetical lists, 12
animation, 67
Apple Computer, 89
architecture, 111
artificial intelligence, 119
ASCII, 51
ASIS, 144
AutoCad, 78
avant-garde, 28

Bank Street College, 30
benefits of hypertext, 22, 25, 29, 108
Bible, 32

bibliographic information systems, 8
biology, 31
bit-mapped images, 70
blueprints, 111
boolean expressions, 10, 12
Brown University, 79, 100, 102
BRS Information Technologies, 24
buildings, 111
buttons, 89

Carnegie Mellon University, 83
cartoons, 114
case-sensitivity, 12
CD-ROM, 15
CD-I, 16
chunking, 62

classics, 30
clipboard, 70
Cognetics Corporation, 86, 133
cognitive load, 9, 10, 11, 63
color, 37, 38
Columbia-Presbyterian Hospital, 24
command languages, 11, 37, 66
computer assisted instruction, 101
concordance, 12
conferences, 109
connectivity, 63
consistency, 63
consultants, 123
context dependent, 80
context sensitivity, 28

contracts, 53
copyright, 53
cross references, 3, 22, 25, 114
crossword puzzles, 113
CSILE project, 30
cut and paste, 70

data entry, 66
data integrity, 42
database management
     systems, 7
desktop publishing, 69, 89
diagnosis, 23
DIALOG, 8, 16, 51
digital storage, 15
digitization, 52, 66, 70
disorientation, 6, 49, 61
distributed networks, 41
Document Examiner, 29
DynamicDesign, 32, 86

Electronic conferencing, 73
Electronic mail, 73
engineering workstations, 38
engineering, 111
English, 31
entrepreneurs, 122
equipment repair, 110
errors, 37, 121
expert systems, 94, 120

formatting, 39, 68
freedom, 2, 10

game, adventure, 25
geographical differences, 113
granularity, 5
graphics standards, 37
Grolier, 16, 22
Greek civilization, 30

Harvard Medical School, 24
Harvard University, 30
heuristic, 121

Holocaust, 33
human factors, 92
hypermedia, 3, 23
HyperTalk, 64, 90

icons, 68
IFIPS, 144
incidental learning, 2
inferences, 119
information retrieval systems,
     8, 51
interactive fiction, 6, 27
involvement, 33, 77

job aids, 111
Johns Hopkins Hospital, 24

keywords, 13, 22, 49, 91
Knowledge Garden, Inc., 94

learning, 72, 100
learning mechanisms, 120
legal documents, 113
libraries, 51–54, 77–79
Library of Congress, 8
limitations of hypertext, 27,
     111
links,
     activation of, 5
     direction of, 4
     flexibility of, 7
     hierarchical, 4
     location in document of, 3
     meaningfulness of, 23
LISP, 82
lobbies, 109

mainframes, 123
margin notes, 32, 41
MCC, 103
McDonnell Douglas, 78, 101
measurement, 56
medical diagnosis, 23
memory aid, 14

mental models, 72
menus, 37, 86
Microsoft, 16
Mitre Corporation, 110
modularity, 6
mouse, 11, 65, 84, 101
Museum of Jewish Heritage, 33

NASA, 29, 110
natural-language programs, 119
New York Times, 8
nirvana, 115
nodes,
     composites of, 6
     size of, 5
     typed, 5
Northern Lights Software, 91
novice users, 9
NTERGAID, 92

object-oriented images, 70
Office Workstations Limited
     (OWL), 88
online reference manuals, 28
optical character recognition,
     52
orientations, 109
outline processors, 45, 101
Oxford English Dictionary, 21

page marking, 14
pagination, 69
Palenque project, 30
parallel processing, 39
passwords, 50
Perseus project, 30
pop-up notes, 5
print, weakness of, 22
product liability, 53
program documentation, 31

query languages, 8, 10

read-only storage, 15

readability, 9, 38, 56, 38
relational databases, 8
repair manual, 29
resolution, 37
response time, 39
resumes, 109, 125
reversibility, 11, 15
royalties, 115

San Diego, 109
Savings Zone Club, 25
SCORPIO, 8
scratchpad, 70
script, 64, 89
scrolling, 9, 65
search algorithms, 13, 43
Seaside Software, 93
semantic differential, 56
semantic information, 119
semantic network, 72
serendipity, 2
shelf space, 22
shopping malls, 109

Smalltalk, 86
Smithsonian Museum, 33
software development tools, 101
specialization, 112
SRI International, 78
stack, 89
standards, 37, 42
Stanford Research Institute, 101
stretch text, 100
Symbolics, Inc, 29

table of contents, 11
tax forms, 123
teaching, 31
Tektronix, 86
time-sharing, 41
touch screen, 11, 65
travel guides, 109
tree structures, 7
truth maintenance, 120

University of Canterbury, 88

University of Maryland, 71, 86, 104
University of North Carolina, 27, 88, 139
University of Toronto, 30
UNIX, 78, 88
updates, 40
U.S. Patent Office, 8
usability laboratories, 56
user control, 121
user empowerment, 121

virtual copy, 50
voice input, 66
VW Rabbit, 29

Washington University, 23
web, 80
word processing, 68
word recognition systems, 66

Xerox, 82, 103

ZOG, 83